DOG CARE FOR PUPPIES

DOG CARE FOR PUPPIES

A Guide to Feeding, Playing, Grooming, and Behavior

Vanessa Charbonneau

ROCKRIDGE
PRESS

Interior and Cover Designer: Karmen Lizzul
Art Producer: Michael Hardgrove
Editor: Lauren O'Neal
Interior art used under license from © iStockphoto.com
Author photo courtesy of © Tiffany Wilson Pet Photography

ISBN: Print 978-1-64739-263-5
eBook 978-1-64739-264-2
R0

To those who choose food over fear.

contents

Introduction

Welcome to this comprehensive puppy care guide, and congratulations on the addition of your new four-legged family member. This is an exciting and busy time in your life as you embark on your journey as a new (or repeat) puppy parent!

I've been around dogs my entire life. My father had a career as a service dog handler with the police force, and watching him work with his canine partner is what motivated my decision to pursue a career involving animals. I started off working in a vet clinic as a registered veterinary technologist (RVT), educating clients on preventive and routine health care, assisting in surgery, and more. I studied animal behavior for two years as part of my RVT training. That experience led me to become a certified dog trainer and business owner, enabling me to educate clients on healthy social development, puppy manners, preventive training, and more.

As a vet tech, I've trained in routine, preventive, and emergency care for puppies and other animals. As a certified dog trainer, I've studied how puppies grow, develop, and learn, and I'm responsible for teaching my clients how to give their puppies the best start to life. Approaching puppies from these two knowledge bases has given me a unique ability to provide guidance and support. In this book, I'll share my knowledge and experience in hopes that it will make your early puppy days, and all those that follow, smooth and enjoyable.

Puppies are blank slates. They have so much potential, but they need our guidance and support to ensure they become balanced adult dogs. I strive to teach my clients a proactive approach. By supporting their puppies in healthy growth and development, owners decrease the likelihood of behavioral problems and increase the positive bond between themselves and their dogs.

I've had the honor of living with a couple of special dogs so far in my life. Each dog has positively impacted me in ways I never would've imagined. The bond you develop with your dog is like no other and can bring so much joy to your life. You and your new puppy will be able to provide each other with love and trust that will grow in strength the more time you share together.

You can read this book before your puppy comes home in preparation for what's to come, but keep it within reach as you start your journey, too, so you can reference it when you encounter something challenging or new. It will help you feel informed, equipped, and confident on your journey to raising the perfect puppy!

CHAPTER 1

Puppy Prep

T he first step on this new adventure isn't bringing your puppy home—it's getting ready. Spending time educating yourself, planning, and preparing your home for your puppy's arrival is the best way to transition into puppy ownership for both you and your new pet. This chapter will help you do just that.

The Right Time for a Puppy

So you're thinking about adding a puppy to your family, but you're unsure when to do it. A pet will impact major areas of your life, like your schedule and finances, so there are a few considerations to keep in mind. First, a stable work schedule is important so you can plan your puppy's feeding and bathroom routine around your work hours. Does your job give you the flexibility needed to let your puppy outside during the day to go to the bathroom, or will you need to hire a dog walker or pet sitter to assist with this? Does your schedule allow additional time to devote to your puppy's exercise and social needs? Puppies require a lot of time, attention, and guidance, especially in the early months, so you must be willing to prioritize them daily. Having funds set aside for regular feeding, grooming, and health care is also important, as are emergency funds for potential accidents or illnesses.

I don't recommend giving puppies as surprise gifts, no matter how adorable they are. Puppies aren't like a new pair of jeans; you can't just return them if you don't like the color or they don't fit you perfectly. A puppy is a lifelong commitment, and you should give it careful thought when deciding whether to add one to your home.

Where to Get Your Puppy

Where do puppies come from? There are several ways you can go about obtaining a puppy, and it's important to understand the pros and cons of each option.

Shelters

An animal shelter is a place that accepts lost, abandoned, or surrendered animals and provides health care and lodging with the goal of eventually finding them homes. An animal shelter might be your local pound or a nonprofit organization such as the Society for the Prevention of Cruelty to Animals (SPCA). When you adopt a puppy from a shelter, you're saving the lives of two animals: the one you're adopting and the next dog to occupy the kennel space you're freeing up. Shelter adoption fees generally include your puppy's vaccinations, deworming, spay or neuter surgery, and a form of permanent ID such as a tattoo or microchip. Adoption fees are generally much lower than a purchase fee from a registered dog breeder, which makes shelter puppies a more financially feasible option.

Shelters are preferable to other options in many ways, but finding a puppy at a shelter might be more difficult, as they're generally in higher demand than adult or senior dogs. The same goes for finding a purebred; most shelters have mixed-breed dogs and/or unclear information on the breeding of their dogs. Also, keep in mind that these animals might have been removed from abusive or negligent living situations, and a traumatic history can impact any animal's social development and behavior.

Rescues

Rescues differ from shelters in that they're privately owned facilities that deal with animals who have been surrendered by their owners or transferred there from animal shelters. Rescues typically place the animals in their care in foster homes, as opposed to the group environment of shelters. Being raised in a home helps the animals become accustomed to this type of lifestyle and provides them with regular social opportunities. Foster homes also tend to have more insight into the personality of the specific puppy you're looking to adopt, which can be helpful when trying to find the right match for you. In addition, rescues can be breed- and age-specific with the animals they care for, which is useful if you have a particular breed of puppy in mind. A rescue might have a more intensive application and interview process than

Say No to Puppy Mills

Puppy mills breed as many puppies as possible in the shortest amount of time for the lowest cost. This results in crowded and unhygienic living conditions, minimal human contact for the dogs, little to no veterinary care, and poor nutrition. Puppy mills are not illegal in most areas, but the conditions these dogs live in often violate local animal cruelty laws. Should your puppy develop a health or behavioral problem as a result of poor breeding or upbringing, puppy mill breeders usually won't let you return them. This can create financial burdens that could potentially be avoided by getting your pet from a safer and more reputable source.

Here are some red flags that indicate you might be acquiring a puppy mill dog.

▶ The puppy is being sold through a pet store, ad, or website.
▶ You're not permitted to view the puppy's parents or living quarters.
▶ The seller offers to deliver the puppy or meet you at a location other than their premises.
▶ There's no contract, interview process, papers, or health history available for the puppy or their parents.

If you're concerned that your dog may be from a puppy mill, you can reach out to your local animal shelter to file a report.

a shelter, which helps ensure you and your chosen puppy are a great match—but it can also be tedious and time-consuming.

When adopting a dog from either a shelter or a rescue, it's important to ask how or why they arrived at the facility. Knowing an animal's history can help you identify areas in which they may require more support when developing. A puppy who was rescued from a puppy mill will likely lack early exposure and socialization opportunities, and they may appear fearful. A puppy who has suffered abuse could have fears associated with specific noises, places, or types and appearances of people. These puppies will require patience and more proactive socialization than the average pup, so be sure that you're willing and able to take on this challenge.

Breeders

Choosing to go with a purebred puppy means you can research and select a breed that matches some of the qualities you want in your dog. When getting your puppy from a reputable breeder, you can often meet your puppy's parents, which can provide further insight into the temperament of your puppy as it matures, and you can see the environment in which your puppy was raised, which directly impacts its social development during the early weeks.

Breeding is an unregulated practice, and any person can identify themselves as a breeder, so it's critical to do your research. A reputable dog breeder invests a lot of time in caring for their dogs and finding them the right homes. They're likely devoting time and money to achieving titles at dog shows, and they are typically involved with their breed club (an association of those who fancy a particular breed of dog, organized under a national kennel club, which decides on breed standards and showing regulations). A reputable breeder should be performing genetic and health testing and should provide you with the results of this testing when you purchase a puppy from them.

Purchasing a puppy from a breeder comes with a considerable price tag compared to a shelter's adoption fees, so it's important to budget for that. Remember to ask the breeder what vaccines and deworming the puppy has had, as each breeder will have their own policies.

Other Places

Sometimes you end up with a puppy because a dog belonging to your friend or neighbor unexpectedly has a litter, or you find a litter abandoned on the street. While you may be providing such puppies with a better life, they also have a lot of unknowns. You might not know much about the puppy's breed history, exact age, or temperament. Most of the time, you're acquiring the puppy without any formal contract or paperwork, so you have no protection if something goes wrong with the puppy's health or the puppy isn't a good fit for your family. Having a health exam done by a veterinarian is the most important first step before bringing your puppy home.

Choosing a Puppy

While there's no way to guarantee what kind of dog your puppy will grow into, researching breed traits can increase the likelihood that your puppy will be the right fit for your family. Picking a breed that best suits your personality and lifestyle will help ensure a long and happy life for your chosen puppy.

Breed

Although each puppy is their own individual, there are certain traits that are commonly found in specific breeds. For example, working dogs like border collies or blue heelers can be very rewarding companions if you have a lot of time to spend exercising your dog and providing mental stimulation.

Puppy Paperwork

When you go to purchase your puppy, be prepared for some form of paperwork. Breeders will likely have you sign a purchase contract that encompasses your responsibilities as the puppy's new owner, discusses health guarantees on your puppy, details showing and breeding rights for your puppy, and lays out what should happen if you want to return your puppy. Shelters and rescues will have you sign an adoption agreement stating your responsibilities as the puppy's new owner, dictating that you must spay or neuter your puppy in a timely fashion, and having you agree to follow-up home visits or checkups. This contract will also likely discuss what to do if you end up not keeping your puppy. Read through any contracts thoroughly and ask questions before signing them. Be wary of contracts that discourage you from contacting the organization if you have concerns about your puppy. Reputable sources will want to support the animals they're placing in communities.

If, however, you don't have that kind of time, these dogs can easily get bored, which may translate into undesirable behavior. Family-friendly dogs like Labradors and retrievers can be good if you have kids, but they can struggle to control their over-the-top excitement around people. Small-breed dogs can be well suited to small living spaces such as condos or apartments—but that doesn't mean they don't need exercise. Terriers, for example, require significant exercise to keep them content.

Something else to consider is your potential puppy's coat (see page 76 for more information). Do you mind hair on your clothing and furniture or having to brush your dog's coat daily? Some breeds, such as poodles, bichons frises, and schnauzers, are considered low-shedding, but they often require regular grooming appointments to maintain their coat. It's also important to know if the puppy you've chosen

has hair or fur, as fur is generally more of a concern for people with allergies.

Will it bother you if your dog barks or howls a lot? Notoriously chatty breeds include beagles, terriers, huskies, and miniature schnauzers, to name a few.

If you have kids, choosing a puppy with a high prey drive or herding instinct, like a border collie or Shetland sheepdog, can pose some unique challenges. Fast movement is extremely stimulating for these types of dogs, so be prepared to manage your puppy around your children.

You should also be aware of local breed bans or restrictions in your area. Some cities have restrictions for dogs who fit into the "bully breed" category, such as pit bulls and mastiffs. They may need to be leashed or muzzled in public, and they may not be allowed in some living spaces or dog parks.

Temperament

Of course, a puppy's breed can only tell you so much—you also need to evaluate their personality. Recognizing specific behaviors and character traits is important for ensuring you make the right choice for yourself. Confident puppies will approach you without hesitation, using normal attention-soliciting behavior such as licking your face. If startled by a loud noise or something unfamiliar, they should recover quickly and be curious about this novelty. Confident puppies are great to own because they're easier to socialize and adjust better to new experiences during their puppyhood.

Shy puppies, on the other hand, may approach you hesitantly or not at all. They startle more easily and take more time to recover. These puppies can still make great pets, but they require a patient and gentle owner who won't rush them or force them into interactions they're not comfortable with. They may take longer to acclimate to new things and be more difficult to socialize. If a puppy warns you by growling or snapping, that might indicate potential aggressive tendencies. A diligent and proactive approach can not only prevent the puppy from practicing these behaviors but also address their underlying motivations and help set them up for success.

Health

While a puppy's health status can never be guaranteed, you can look for signs that your prospective puppy is in good health while you're visiting them in a familiar environment before adopting. Do they move normally, or do they stumble and not use all four paws properly? Are they engaging with the other puppies and you, or are they lying quietly by themselves? The puppy should have a good appetite and normal energy levels without signs of lethargy, no discharge or redness in the eyes or nose, and clean ears that are free of wax or debris. Check the puppy's coat to ensure it's free of dirt and detritus, with no obvious odor. Ask if the puppy has been experiencing any coughing, sneezing, vomiting, or diarrhea.

If you do select a puppy who shows signs of potential health problems, make sure you're prepared for the financial responsibility that will accompany them. Have your puppy checked by a vet right away, ideally before you even bring them home, in case their condition is contagious to you or other animals. For many health issues, early intervention can make the difference between a successful recovery and a lengthy medical battle.

Puppy-Proofing

Before you bring your new pet home, you'll want to prepare your house, yard, and car to ensure your stuff is safe from your puppy—and your puppy is safe from your stuff. Preparing yourself ahead of time will set you and your puppy up for success right off the bat.

Your House

Puppies explore the world with their mouths, and this includes your home and everything in it. Anything within your puppy's reach can quickly become a chew toy. Placing chewable items behind a closed door, in a closet, or on a high shelf can prevent your puppy from accessing and destroying them. Remember: They might not be able to reach certain places when they're small, but as they grow taller, their reach will be higher.

If you can't put something out of reach (e.g., your couch), you should only allow your puppy supervised access to the room that contains that item. Supervised access means constant supervision; always keep your eyes on your puppy while they're in the space.

Here are some common measures to puppy-proof your house.

▶ Cover electrical cords with a cord cover or prevent your puppy from chewing them.

▶ Store your trash in a can with a lid that locks or inside a cupboard. A curious puppy can quickly figure out how to flip open a cupboard door, so use child locks. Close bathroom doors or safely contain their trash cans in a similar fashion.

▶ Keep houseplants out of reach, as puppies find plants fun to chew on and dig up! Search online to see if your houseplants are toxic to your puppy, and if they are, replace them or put them in rooms the puppy doesn't have access to.

▶ Smaller items, such as tissue boxes, TV remotes, books, and electronics, are common objects for puppies to chew, so keep them safely out of reach.

▶ Blankets and other textiles are fun to chew or shred, so tuck them away in a closet.

Your Yard

If you have a yard, it'll likely be a place where your puppy will spend a lot of time exploring, playing, and relieving themselves. Here are some standard ways to puppy-proof a yard.

▶ Look up the plants in your yard online to check if they're toxic to dogs. If they are, they should be removed or protected behind a fence.

▶ Chemicals like fertilizers, pesticides, and antifreeze need to be locked away so your puppy doesn't accidentally ingest them.

- Walk the perimeter of your yard, ensuring your fence is in good condition with no holes or potential escape routes. Check that the latches on your gates close securely.
- Secure your garden beds and planters to prevent your puppy from accessing them. Garden beds make for excellent digging, so putting a small fence around them is a good idea.
- Remember, anything can become a chew toy to your puppy, including gravel, stones, scraps of wood, or garden tools. If you don't want your puppy to chew or swallow something, lock it up outside their reach.
- Supervising your puppy during their first few times out in the yard is recommended, as many puppies prove to be very skilled at digging under or climbing over seemingly secure fences.

Your Car

When you go to pick up your puppy, you want to be ready for that first car ride home! A loose puppy can quickly wreak havoc in a vehicle. Here are a few things to consider before transporting your pup.

- A crate is the safest way to transport your puppy in a vehicle. Secure your crate in the vehicle with bungees or seatbelt anchors so it doesn't move around during travel.
- If a crate doesn't fit in your car, a pet seatbelt can help contain your puppy.
- Install seat covers or a "dog hammock" to protect your vehicle's upholstery from claws, hair, and dirt. Choosing a washable option makes it easier to clean and maintain your vehicle!
- Remember, anything your puppy can reach, they can chew, so remove any clutter and don't leave your puppy in your vehicle unsupervised.

Picking Up Your Puppy

It's finally time to go pick up your new puppy! This is an exciting time, but it's not something you want to rush into unprepared. Getting everything organized beforehand can result in a much smoother transition for your puppy—and you.

Puppy Prep Checklist

Earlier, we discussed puppy-proofing your home. Now let's dive into puppy-*prepping* your home! Here are the things you should have ready before you pick up your puppy.

- ☐ **A crate.** If you're going to crate-train your puppy, set up the crate before they arrive in the room where they'll sleep. Place a blanket in the crate and have extra blankets handy (in the event of potty-training accidents).
- ☐ **Food and water bowls.**
- ☐ **Food.** Speak with the person you're purchasing your puppy from about what food they're currently using so you can either purchase the same brand or bring enough of it home to gradually transition your puppy onto a new diet.
- ☐ **A variety of toys.** These will give your puppy something to play with so they won't need to use your furniture or shoes as chew toys.
- ☐ **Cleaning supplies.** Be prepared for potty-training accidents with an enzymatic cleaner made by brands such as Rocco & Roxie Supply Co. or Nature's Miracle. These sprays use enzymes to break down organic material so you can clean messes thoroughly and prevent any lingering odor. (Your puppy is more likely to have repeat accidents in the same spot if they can smell they've gone there before.)

- ☐ **A leash.** Six feet is a good standard length. I advise going with a cheap nylon leash at first, as puppies like to chew things, and leashes are no exception. It will be much less frustrating if your puppy chews through a $10 nylon leash than a $40 leather leash.

- ☐ **A collar.** Make sure to purchase a collar that will fit around your puppy's small neck. Choose an inexpensive one to start, as your puppy will more than likely outgrow it and require an upgrade (or five).

- ☐ **An ID tag.** This tag should display your puppy's name and your phone number—too much more information can be hard to read. Your puppy should have this tag on them at all times in case they ever manage to escape. An additional microchip or tattoo gives your puppy the best chance of being returned to you.

- ☐ **Baby gates.** If you don't want your puppy to have access to the entire house, you can put up baby gates to keep them out of certain areas. Set these up (or close the doors to off-limits rooms) before you bring your puppy home.

What to Bring

Don't leave to pick up your new puppy empty-handed! Be prepared with the necessary supplies. Here are some items you should bring with you.

- ☐ **A leash.**
- ☐ **A collar.**
- ☐ **A crate** (if that's how you are going to transport your puppy in the vehicle).
- ☐ **A blanket** for the puppy to rest on, in or out of the crate.
- ☐ **Tasty treats** to help you make a good first impression!
- ☐ **Food and water** if you'll be traveling for a long period.

First Things First

When you first meet your puppy, try to act calm and avoid any over-the-top excitement, which can elicit a similar response from your puppy. Crouch down so you're closer to the puppy's level and let them sniff your hand before attempting to pet them. You can feed your puppy treats when they approach and interact with you or for any good behavior you notice, such as sitting politely to be pet. If your puppy is unsure about getting in the car, you can lure them in with treats or gently pick them up if the step is too high. If your puppy balks at the vehicle, stop, take a moment to settle them, then gently encourage them forward using praise and treats.

Once you arrive home, the very first thing you'll want to do is give your puppy an opportunity to go to the bathroom. This is a great time to introduce your puppy to the designated "potty spot" in your yard and reward them for eliminating there.

Next, show your puppy where to find their water dish, toys, and crate or bed. You can let your puppy explore the house, but make sure you're actively supervising so they don't make any bad choices.

Introductions

Just like there are rules when we introduce ourselves to other humans, there are rules for introducing puppies to the people and animals they'll be living with. First impressions matter for animals, too, so positive introductions can go a long way in building healthy relationships.

You can monitor how your puppy is doing by reading their body language (see page 29). If things are going well, they should act relaxed, with a loose, wagging tail; ears neutral or forward; and a soft mouth. It's a good sign if your puppy is approaching the novel person or animal of their own accord, rather than hiding or trying to leave the space.

If things aren't going well, your puppy will show fearful body language: a tense, closed mouth or excessive panting/ yawning; cowering or rolling over to expose their belly; tail tucked between their legs or upright and stiff; avoiding eye contact; trying to leave, escape, or hide. For a dog, growling or snarling is a clear way of saying, "Give me space! Don't come any closer." If your puppy shows fearful behavior, remove them from the situation for the time being by putting either the puppy or the other animal/person in a different room with a barrier, such as a baby gate or closed door, between them.

Meeting Kids

When introducing your new puppy to kids, especially young kids, be careful not to overwhelm the puppy. Have the kids sit quietly on the floor and instruct them to be calm and quiet with their voices—no screaming, fighting, or speaking over one another. Don't have the kids approach the dog. Instead, allow the puppy to approach the kids one at a time.

If the puppy is happy to greet the child, let the child pet the dog gently three times on the chest or shoulder area. After these three pets, have the child stop and wait to see what the puppy does. Do they solicit further attention from the child? If so, the two are welcome to continue interacting. If the puppy moves away, the child should allow this to happen and not pursue the puppy. If they want to play with the puppy (and the puppy seems agreeable to this idea), have them use a toy, rather than their hands or body, in order to avoid play biting.

Meeting Other Dogs

If you have another dog in the house, don't necessarily expect them to tolerate this new, energetic puppy right away. The first introduction between the two should be supervised and controlled. Have the puppy on a leash so they can't jump all over your other dog, and don't be alarmed if your older dog warns the new puppy with a growl or a snap. Puppies are still developing appropriate social skills and don't yet know all the rules or boundaries. The older dog will be working to establish these rules, and growling is a form of communication.

Keep interactions short and sweet at the beginning to avoid overwhelming either dog. Start off letting them interact while separated by baby gates or with one dog in a crate or pen so they can acclimate to each other's presence without being pressured to interact directly. Advocate for both dogs: If the older dog is clearly trying to communicate to the puppy

that they've had enough playing and the puppy doesn't take the hint, either remove the puppy or provide the older dog with an escape route.

Meeting Cats and Other Pets

Before you introduce your dog to another non-dog animal, make sure to familiarize yourself with that animal's body language. It's important to be able to recognize if the other animal feels threatened or uncomfortable so you can decide if the introduction should continue. If you own a cat, you'll need to be careful about initial introductions. Even a young puppy might already be larger than a cat and could accidentally injure them by playing too roughly—and, conversely, cats have sharp claws, which your puppy probably isn't anticipating. Cats also tend to flee from danger, which can encourage a puppy to engage in a game of chase that will be very fun for the puppy but not for the cat.

For the first introduction to your family cat, keep your puppy on a leash or confined to a crate. Allow the cat to approach at their own leisure, never forcing the pets to interact if they don't want to. Watching the body language of both the puppy and the cat will give you insight into whether they're enjoying the interaction or getting stressed out. Allow the two to adjust to each other over time by gradually increasing exposure (with barriers in place for the puppy, such as a crate, baby gate, or leash). Always ensure that your cat has a hiding place that the puppy can't access. Reward any calm and quiet behavior that you observe from your puppy here; this encourages the puppy to offer this same type of behavior when they're around the cat in the future.

As for "pocket pets" such as mice, rats, hamsters, and guinea pigs, they're not meant to interact with dogs, and it's crucial that any interactions are always supervised and under your full control. In fact, there's really no reason to allow your puppy to interact with your pocket pet at all, so make sure the pocket pet lives in a secure cage that your puppy can't access or break into.

CHAPTER 2

Your New Best Friend

As you get to know your new puppy, it's important to understand the rapid development and growth taking place in their initial weeks through their first few years of life. Knowing what your puppy is going through can help you take a proactive approach to care and training, reducing frustration for both of you.

As Your Puppy Grows

Each stage of life brings new milestones for puppies. Let's look at the various stages of growth, what's occurring during each one, and what you can expect to witness, both physically and socially, as your puppy matures.

0 to 2 weeks

Your puppy is considered a "neonate" (newborn) at this stage and is completely dependent on their mother for everything, including nutrition, hygiene, and elimination. Puppies will snuggle next to their mom and "heap" on top of one another to keep warm, as they can't regulate their body temperatures yet. Their eyes and ears are closed, so they're learning about their world entirely through touch and smell—but at this age, puppies can only move by crawling, so they're not doing much exploration. They spend most of the day nursing, sleeping, and growing.

Don't Take Your Puppy Home Too Soon!

The most important thing to know about your puppy's early development is that *they shouldn't leave their mother before 8 weeks of age.* Puppies require diligent, around-the-clock care during these critical weeks, and they learn a lot from their mothers and littermates. Early removal from the litter might result in a puppy who's less capable of adapting to new situations later in life. Studies show that puppies who are removed from their mothers before 8 weeks are more prone to attention-seeking behaviors, reactivity to noises, fearfulness on walks, excessive barking, aversion to strangers, and inappropriate play biting.

2 to 4 weeks

This is considered the transitional phase in a puppy's development. Their eyes and ears open, and their senses are rapidly developing. Their teeth start to emerge, although they won't become a full set of baby teeth until 6 to 8 weeks of age. Your puppy is becoming increasingly mobile, learning to walk at around 3 weeks of age. Walking is followed by scampering and other faster, albeit clumsy, movements. Puppies are also now learning to bark, wag their tails, and communicate with one another. Soon they'll be able to eliminate on their own without their mom's help.

4 to 8 weeks

During this time, puppies start to nurse less and less, until eventually they wean off mother's milk completely. That means they'll start eating solid foods like soft puppy food and eventually kibble. There is a steep increase in their motor skills and function in this period, as most of their waking hours are spent playing with littermates. Through this play, puppies develop and rehearse various social skills and learn "bite inhibition" (not applying too much pressure with their teeth). Although they're becoming more independent, it's important that puppies stay with their mom and littermates until they're 8 weeks of age at a minimum. Removing the puppy too soon can interfere with important social development.

8 to 16 weeks

This is when you're likely bringing your new puppy home. It's important to know that they're now in what we call the "socialization period," which plays a crucial role in shaping their future personality. The critical socialization period is between 3 and 12 weeks, but socialization deficits through 14 weeks of age can lead to behavioral issues later on. Your puppy is learning by association, so use treats and patience to make sure that all interactions and experiences they have during this time are positive and fun! Simultaneously, between 8 and 11 weeks of age, your puppy may experience their first fear period, where novel stimuli may alarm or spook them. During this stage, it's important to try to protect your puppy from frightening experiences, as they can leave a permanent mark. Don't pressure them to approach or interact with anything they're nervous about, and use rewards to make new experiences positive for them.

4 to 12 months

Your puppy's socialization period ends around 12 to 14 weeks of age—but that doesn't mean you can sit back and rest. Continuing to expose your dog to the world and new experiences, at the dog's pace and in a positive way, is important during their entire first year so that they can practice learned behaviors in new environments.

At around 6 months, your puppy is now considered an adolescent, whether they've become sexually mature or not. This is a busy and active phase of life in which they continue to work on developing and maturing their social skills. Regular interactions and play with other dogs keep their social skills sharp and can also be a great outlet for their abundance of energy at this age. Regular obedience and manners training can help make these busy dogs manageable and more enjoyable to be around, while also tiring out their brains. Mental stimulation can prevent boredom and the behavior problems that go with it.

Puppy Puberty

Your dog may hit sexual maturity as early as 5 months of age, although, with larger breeds, it can take well over a year or even 2 years in giant breeds. At that point, your dog is considered reproductively viable and is technically no longer a puppy. As with humans, your dog will experience a massive shift in hormones during puberty, which can result in some big behavioral changes, such as urine marking in males (and sometimes females); mounting or humping other dogs, people, or objects; increased attraction to "intact" dogs (dogs that aren't spayed or neutered); and an increase in wandering and roaming behavior. In most breeds, intact, sexually mature female dogs "go into heat" twice a year, meaning they're in the fertile part of their reproductive cycle and can get pregnant. This is usually characterized by vaginal discharge/bleeding for up to 18 days, but female dogs are most fertile during the last 4 to 5 days of estrus, when bleeding is at the lowest level. Be sure to take precautions to prevent unwanted breeding during this time.

Spaying or neutering your dog can prevent these undesirable behaviors as well as accidental pregnancies. Speak to your veterinarian about the best time to have your pet spayed or neutered.

1 to 2 years

Around 18 months of age, your dog may start testing the boundaries of known cues or commands. I jokingly call this the "juvenile delinquent" phase of life. In other words, your dog is now a teenager! This may come with certain behavioral changes. You may notice a shift in your dog's overall sociability anytime between 1 and 3 years of age. They might be more selective about whom they play with, what kind of play they tolerate freely, or their desire to play in general. These are normal changes and will vary for each dog.

Canine Communication

Humans have been coexisting with dogs for millennia, but until recently, we didn't focus much on communication between dogs and people. Humans rely primarily on verbal communication, whereas dogs do most of their communicating with body language. It's important for us to recognize how dogs use their bodies to communicate—and what they're trying to say.

How Your Puppy Talks to You

Dogs communicate largely with their bodies, and some of their signs are often subtle, overlooked, or misinterpreted. When evaluating a dog's body language, look at the big picture, not just one body part. The same body language can have various meanings, depending on the context and other signs it's paired with.

Eyes

A happy puppy should have soft, neutral eyes, while a puppy who is alert, angry, or excited might look at you with a "hard stare" involving dilated pupils and very little blinking. A dog who is nervous or anxious might look at you in a sideways fashion so that you see the whites of their eyes. This is called a "whale eye," and a dog displaying this signal needs space.

Ears

Your puppy's ears can give you a lot of insight into their emotional state. Forward, alert ears could indicate conflict, interest, or aggression. Ears that are held back indicate fear or worry. Looking at your puppy's ears in the context of other body language will help you identify their meaning.

Mouth

Panting is the universal signal for a hot dog, but did you know it can also indicate stress? On the other hand, a mouth that is tightly closed can mean fear or anxiety; a dog doing this should be handled with caution. Snarling, growling, a curled lip, or bared teeth are all clear indicators that your puppy is not happy, and you should stop whatever it is you're doing to prevent escalating their response to a possible bite. A happy puppy has a soft and relaxed mouth.

Body Posture

A dog standing forward with their weight on their front legs might be feeling defensive, whereas a dog with their weight primarily on their hind legs is worried and not very confident. A dog who is cowering or crouched down low is scared. Raised "hackles" (the hairs along a dog's neck and back) indicate fear or arousal. Some dogs roll over to show you their belly in hopes of tummy rubs, but it can also be a sign of fear or submission: "Don't hurt me, I'm not a threat!" This dog may or may not want to be touched, so look for other cues to help you decide the appropriate action. A "play bow," when the dog gets down on its elbows with its butt in the air, is the signal for "Let's play!"

Tail

A wagging tail is commonly thought to indicate a happy, friendly dog, but dogs can also wag their tails when they're angry. Tail posture is important to consider here: A stiff, upright, wagging tail signals a dog who is defensive or angry, whereas a loose, floppy wag suggests this dog is happy to meet you. A tail that is low or tucked under the dog's belly indicates fear.

Verbal

Dogs do use some verbal communication, such as barking, whining, or howling. Depending on context, these can indicate anything from pain to distress to excitement. Be mindful of the conversation your dog is trying to have with you. A growl is usually a warning, and it's important to evaluate why the dog feels the need to warn you and to manipulate the environment to help alleviate the conflict.

How You Talk to Your Puppy

Unfortunately, we don't speak dog, but with some education, you can communicate clearly with your puppy. While dogs don't speak, we can teach them to understand many words. Puppies don't come preprogrammed to know what "Sit" or "Down" mean, yet most dogs learn these cues over their lives and respond to them appropriately. Dogs are also good at learning hand signals and are very responsive to audio signals from devices like clickers. As dogs communicate with one another primarily through body language, they also become good at reading ours. When you're angry, does your dog react by looking "guilty" or submissive? If so, this is a response to your body language. I always encourage dog owners to take a proactive approach instead of a reactive one. Set your dog up for success! Teach your dog what you want from them right from the beginning. Dogs do what works, and we can use this to our advantage.

Communication via Consequences

Dogs learn by association, particularly from the consequences associated with their actions. If a behavior is rewarded or reinforced, that behavior is likely going to happen more frequently. If a behavior is not rewarded, its frequency will decrease.

Communicate what you like from your puppy by rewarding them with praise, toys, play, and treats. If your puppy is doing something you don't like, try to find a replacement behavior. For example, if your dog jumps up on you when they want to play, don't pet them or push them off, as this is very rewarding—you gave them the attention they were seeking. Instead, ask your puppy to do something more appropriate, such as "Sit," and then reward that desirable behavior with petting or a game of tug-of-war.

Punishment, such as yelling or physical reprimands, may seem like a helpful tool, but it's actually highly unnecessary. Forcefully telling your dog "No!" doesn't help them learn what they should be doing. In fact, it doesn't even necessarily tell them what they did was wrong. (They don't speak human languages!) Instead, this can scare your puppy, damaging the bond you've worked so hard to form. If your puppy develops a negative association with you, it will only make them harder to train and can cause more behavioral problems. Communicating in a way they can understand, with real learning, is a much better option.

Common Misunderstandings

Humans and dogs are different species, so it's no surprise that we don't always understand each other. Here are a few common misunderstandings you'll want to clear up for the optimal relationship with your new best friend.

Myth #1: Alpha Dogs

The dominance theory is one myth that just won't quit. Owners commonly think that if they don't assert dominance over their dog, their dog will think it's the "alpha dog" and therefore in charge. This is simply not true. The research that originally gave us these concepts has now been cast into doubt because it studied captive wolves in a zoo. More recent studies on wolves in the wild have shown that wolf packs are usually family units and the "alphas" are really just the breeding male and female (or, to put it more simply, the mother and father). One study on free-roaming packs of dogs (not wolves) actually found that a few older, more experienced dogs took turns being the "leader."

In reality, dogs do what works. They don't sleep on couches to show us they're the boss; they sleep there because it's comfortable. If jumping up on visitors results in happy talking and petting, the dog will jump up on the next visitor, and the one after that. They're not trying to show your guests that they're the king of the castle, and forcing your dog into submission won't fix that behavior.

Myth #2: Rub Their Nose in It

Many people are taught that when a dog has a potty-training accident, rubbing its nose in the mess will teach it not to repeat the behavior. This is entirely false. By employing an aversive technique (something your dog finds distasteful or uncomfortable), you're only teaching the dog that you are unpredictable and scary. Furthermore, you might inadvertently teach your dog that it's not safe to eliminate in front of you and that they should therefore sneak away to perform their business where you can't see them. If you find your dog eliminating in the house, interrupt them by calmly picking them up or ushering them outside and then reward the behavior if they continue to eliminate outside. An even better, more proactive approach would be to prevent accidents from occurring in the first place by increasing your supervision and providing more frequent bathroom breaks.

Myth #3: You Can't Teach an Old Dog New Tricks

As a dog trainer, I'm frequently asked by clients if their dog is "too old" to be trained or attend classes. My answer is always a resounding no! Your dog is never too old to learn, be trained, or modify their behavior. In fact, mental exercise through training and other activities can be extremely beneficial to senior dogs and can slow their cognitive decline. When training with any dog, but particularly an older dog, be conscious of their physical limitations. Train on stable, non-slippery footing and allow frequent "brain breaks."

CHAPTER 3

Food and Nutrition

Nutrition is important for your growing puppy, and the mass of dog food options on the market can be overwhelming. This chapter will cover the basics of what your puppy needs to grow healthy and strong while also helping you choose feeding options that fit your lifestyle.

What to Feed Your Puppy

There are a few different ways to approach feeding your puppy, and each has its advantages and disadvantages. This section will guide you through your decision-making process, helping you choose the best option for your puppy and you. It's important to select a pet food based on your puppy's age and phase of growth, keeping any medical concerns in mind. Consult with your veterinarian about your food selection to ensure it meets your puppy's needs.

Dry Kibble

Kibble is the most common choice for feeding puppies and adult dogs. It's low-cost, has a long shelf life, and doesn't require any special storage. It also has the added benefit of massaging your puppy's gums and teeth to a degree, which can contribute to improved oral health. There is a large variety of options available on the market, but not all are equally appropriate for your puppy.

When choosing a kibble brand, check first for an AAFCO certification label on the bag. This indicates that the product has undergone testing and feeding trials by the Association of American Feed Control Officials and has been deemed balanced and appropriate for use.

Next, consider the ingredient list on the back of the bag. Dogs, unlike cats, are not strict carnivores. Plant-based ingredients like grains, fruits, and vegetables are not just dietary fillers; they contain important vitamins, minerals, and fiber that contribute to your puppy's overall health and development. That said, a protein should be one of the first three ingredients listed.

You'll also want to research the manufacturer and company to ensure you're buying a reputable brand with good quality-control measures. Veterinary-exclusive brands, such

Going Grain-Free?

A popular trend as of late is grain-free dog foods. Dogs, unlike their wolf ancestors, have evolved with modified genes that allow them to digest carbohydrates with ease. Dogs may do well on grain-free diets, but from a metabolic standpoint, they don't need them. Some owners choose these diets if they're concerned about grain allergies, but proteins like chicken and beef are more common allergens.

as Medi-Cal, Hill's, or Science Diet, are among my top brand recommendations for their rigorous research, feeding trials, and quality-control practices, but there are plenty of other great options out there.

Wet Food

Wet, or canned, food often has the same ingredients as kibble but in different ratios. For example, wet food is of course much higher in water than kibble. Canned food is packaged in durable containers and generally has a long shelf life, but once it's opened, it must be refrigerated and fed to your puppy within a few days or it'll go bad. Wet food is often more palatable to dogs, so it may be a better choice for a picky eater. However, it's also more expensive than kibble. If you're looking to both save money and add flavor, try mixing a few tablespoons of a yummy wet food in with your dog's kibble at each meal instead of feeding them wet food alone.

Raw Food

Although it may be an option to look into when your dog is older, raw diets are not recommended for puppies. It's very important for them to get enough calcium and phosphorus as they grow, and if the raw diet is not appropriately balanced, it can result in bone deformities and growth issues.

There are also some major health risks to consider. There's no guarantee that these products are free of dangerous pathogens, such as *Salmonella* or *E. coli*, which can cause vomiting, diarrhea, fevers, and occasionally death for dogs. If you or your kids accidentally ingest bacteria like these when preparing and feeding raw meals, when your puppy licks you, or even when scooping your puppy's poop, you could suffer the same consequences. For these reasons, the FDA "does not believe feeding raw pet foods to animals is consistent with the goal of protecting the public from significant health risks."

Get Milk?

By the time you've brought your new puppy home at eight weeks or older, they'll no longer require their mother's milk. Milk is extremely high in fat and sugars, and it really adds no nutritional value to your puppy's diet—plus too much can cause gastrointestinal upset, diarrhea, or vomiting. Milk (including goat milk) can be given as a treat, but only a few tablespoons at a time. If you're worried that your puppy is underweight or not growing enough, consult with your veterinarian. Milk probably isn't the answer.

Homemade Food

Some owners choose to make their own puppy food at home, which can theoretically be fine as long as you ensure that the diet is nutritionally balanced and appropriate for your dog's life stage. The problem is that this is very difficult to do. A team of researchers at UC Davis found that of the 200 homemade dog food recipes they tested, 95 percent lacked "at least one essential nutrient" and over 83 percent had "multiple nutrient deficiencies." Even recipes by veterinarians sometimes fell short. If you do choose to take this route, use recipes created by veterinary *nutritionists*, and don't experiment or stray from the recipe. It's also recommended to consult with and have your puppy's diet evaluated by a veterinary nutritionist. You'll need a food scale to ensure you're using the proper ratios of ingredients and feeding appropriate amounts to your puppy. And remember, you'll

have to adjust the recipe as your puppy grows! Additionally, make sure you cook meat thoroughly to destroy any potential pathogens that can make your pet ill.

Age-Appropriate Food

When choosing a kibble or wet food, you may notice that some are specifically labeled "for puppies" or "all stages." Because they're doing a lot of important growing in their early weeks, puppies have different nutritional requirements than adult dogs. Puppy food takes this into consideration and is formulated for growth. (Despite its name, "all stages" food is still puppy food and usually isn't suitable for adult or senior dogs.)

Puppy food is often acceptable for puppies of all types, but there are some breed-specific considerations to keep in mind, particularly concerning the puppy's size. As you can imagine, a St. Bernard or mastiff puppy is developing a lot more bone than a Chihuahua and will therefore require more calcium and phosphorus. Meanwhile, your Chihuahua might prefer a small-breed food with a kibble size that's easier for tiny mouths to chew.

There are some breed-specific diets for common breeds on the market, as well. For example, Labrador retrievers are

known to gain weight easily, so a Lab-specific diet may be designed with fewer calories per piece of kibble. As always, it's important to consider the health status, energy, and nutritional needs of your specific dog. When in doubt, speak with your vet.

Switching Food

At some point in your puppy's life, you'll likely have to change their diet, whether from puppy to adult food or for health-specific reasons. Regardless of the reason, it's important to change your puppy's food gradually. Switching to a new diet too quickly can result in indigestion, gas, diarrhea, and vomiting. The general rule for transitioning to a new diet is to do it over seven days, slowly reducing the volume of the old food as you simultaneously increase the volume of the new food. On days one and two, you might feed 75 percent old food and 25 percent new food; on days three and four, a 50/50 ratio; and so on until, on day seven, the puppy's meal is 100 percent new food.

How Much to Feed Your Puppy

As with humans, puppies need more food as they grow bigger. How much you feed your puppy at any given life stage depends on many factors: size, age, energy level, exercise level, current weight, and body condition score (a score that determines if your puppy is at the right weight by evaluating factors like their ribs, profile, and overhead view).

Because different foods vary in terms of nutrition and calories, there isn't a standard recommended volume of food per day. Most labels will tell you the food's calorie content per cup and offer suggestions on how much food to give your puppy based on their weight and age. This number usually tells you what your puppy needs over a 24-hour

A Note on Bloat

Gastric dilatation volvulus (GDV), also known as "bloat," is a medical emergency in which a dog's stomach fills with air and twists by up to 360 degrees. This can close off the esophagus, reduce blood supply to the heart, and damage the liver and spleen. Large-breed, deep-chested dogs are more susceptible to GDV, likely because there's more space in their bodies for their stomachs to move around. Signs of bloat include drooling, panting, retching (trying to vomit but not actually producing vomit), lethargy, and a distended abdomen. If you notice any of these symptoms in your dog, you should bring them to a veterinarian immediately. Bloat is a serious and sometimes fatal condition. Early intervention can be lifesaving!

No one's really sure what causes bloat, but it may be correlated with high levels of activity directly after eating or drinking. Try to eliminate stress from mealtime—slow your dog's feeding down with a special "slow feeder" bowl, and avoid exercise or vigorous activity after mealtime. Some veterinarians even recommend a surgical procedure to prevent bloat in more susceptible breeds.

period, so divide it by the number of meals you feed your puppy per day. For example, if your puppy should get 1 cup of food per day, and you feed them three meals a day, you'll feed ⅓ cup at each meal. Puppies generally start out eating three smaller meals per day and then transition to two slightly larger meals per day as they approach the four- to five-month mark.

Note that spaying or neutering a dog will lower their energy requirements slightly, which means they won't need as many calories as they did before. Adjusting your puppy's food proactively after the operation can prevent unnecessary weight gain. (Though it's not as much of a concern in puppies, obesity is a widespread problem in adult dogs and can lead to health issues like diabetes, heart disease, and arthritis.)

Special Diets

Some puppies and dogs have special needs when it comes to what they can and cannot eat. For example, if your puppy has frequent indigestion, your vet might prescribe a gastrointestinal (GI) diet, which is designed to be bland and easily digestible but still nutritionally balanced. (Make sure to buy a puppy formula to continue supporting development.)

Your puppy might also need a special diet if they're allergic to certain foods, like chicken, beef, dairy, or eggs. (Grains and other plant-based foods are less common allergens.) If your dog has itchy or infected skin, ear infections, or gastrointestinal distress, they might have allergies—or they might have parasites or another illness, so be sure to visit your vet. It's difficult to test animals for allergies reliably. The most common technique is a dietary elimination trial in which you feed your dog only foods that *do not* contain the suspected allergen for eight weeks and monitor the results. For example, if you completely remove beef from your dog's diet and notice that their skin gets less red and itchy, your dog may have a sensitivity to beef proteins, and you should only feed them food without beef or beef products (including beef-flavored treats and medications). A vet can help you keep your dog comfortable during a food trial by treating any underlying infections and making sure you aren't inadvertently feeding them the wrong foods. Note that trials can be difficult if you have kids at home, as they may be prone to dropping food on the ground or feeding the dog without your knowledge.

Water

Drinking enough water is just as important for dogs as it is for humans, so your puppy needs access to fresh, clean water daily. Puppies generally require one ounce of water per pound of body weight each day, but that can vary depending on how hot it is outside and how much the dog has exercised. Keep a dish of water in an easily accessible area of your home, ideally one where your puppy spends a lot of time.

Rinse the bowl and replace the water daily to keep it free of gross buildup and dirt, and wash it with soap and water at least once a week.

If you're worried that your puppy may be dehydrated, speak to your veterinarian. Signs of dehydration include dry or tacky gums, sunken or dry eyes, or a persistent "skin tent" (when you pull up the puppy's scruff and it takes several seconds to return to normal). There are some ways you can encourage your puppy to drink more water, such as feeding them wet food or adding a small amount of low-sodium chicken or beef broth to their water.

Supplements

There are many nutritional supplements on the market for dogs, and it can be confusing to know what exactly your dog needs. Common supplements that address specific medical conditions include joint supplements such as glucosamine for adult or senior dogs and fish oils or omega-3 fatty acids to support dry, dull, or itchy skin.

If you're feeding your puppy an appropriate and nutritionally balanced diet, there is usually no need for supplements. Consult with your vet before adding one to your puppy's diet to be certain it's safe and effective. You might need pharmaceuticals to properly address a medical concern, but supplements can often support the treatment or help prevent the problem from reoccurring. And make sure you follow your vet's or the product's guidelines and use the right dose for your puppy's age and weight.

Human Food

It may be tempting to offer your puppy human food, but there are some things to consider first. Remember, if you're feeding your puppy a nutritionally balanced dog food, human food is not needed to support their nutritional health—it probably just adds calories and fats to their daily intake. Many human foods are too rich for puppies, which can result in an upset stomach, vomiting, or diarrhea. And some human foods are unsafe or even toxic for dogs (see page 103). Avoid foods with sauces or spices, since it can be difficult to know exactly what the ingredients are.

Feeding your puppy while cooking or at the dinner table can encourage them to be underfoot or beg. It can be confusing for your dog if one day they're allowed to eat people food at dinnertime, but the next time they ask, you get upset with them for begging. There is, however, one thing human foods can do for puppies: They make excellent high-value training treats.

Meatless Mutts?

Contrary to popular belief, dogs are not carnivores; they're omnivores, meaning they eat both plants and animals. Because of this, dogs can technically survive on a vegetarian or even vegan diet. But vegetarian diets aren't easy. In addition to the potential challenges of getting your puppy to accept meatless food, it becomes trickier to provide a balanced diet with enough protein and other nutrients. The easiest way to achieve this is with commercially available vegetarian options. Homemade versions often fall short, so take care to speak with your veterinarian before trying it. Vegan diets have even fewer suitable protein options and must be approached extremely carefully, if at all.

Treats

Treats are a great way to show affection to dogs, praise them for a job well done, or train them on new skills and behaviors. While giving treats to your dog is okay—and even encouraged in many scenarios—like all good things, it should be done in moderation. Treats are formulated to be tasty and valuable, not wholesome and nutritionally balanced. They shouldn't make up the bulk of your dog's daily caloric intake, and overfeeding can result in excessive weight gain.

Training Treats

Training treats are the same as any other treats but are generally smaller and more "valuable"—that is, extra tasty to your puppy. Your training treats should be roughly pea-sized, even for larger puppies, so that you can feed plenty of them without filling your puppy up on empty calories or upsetting their stomach as you have them try a new behavior over and over.

The more valuable the treat, the more motivated your puppy will be to work for it! Experiment with various types of treats to see what your puppy likes best and reserve those for training only. For dogs, the smellier the better, so what might be an off-putting odor to you is often the jackpot for your dog.

High-Value Training Treats

High-value treats are kind of like the equivalent of ice cream or chocolate to humans (though of course you should never feed chocolate to your puppy or any dog!). Examples include freeze-dried beef liver, tripe, diced pieces of cheese, well-cooked chicken, and hot dogs. They have a *huge* motivational value to your puppy, which makes them the perfect treat for training in highly distracting environments or for particularly difficult behaviors, such as recalls at the dog park. Reserve these treats for difficult training environments so that they don't lose their potency. When training at home or teaching simpler behaviors, stick with moderate-value training treats.

Chew Treats

Puppies explore the world with their mouths, so it makes sense that they love to chew, especially during their teething phase. Chew treats allow puppies to fulfill their chewing instincts in an appropriate way instead of gnawing on your furniture or shoes.

Choose a chew treat that's durable enough to last a while but not so hard that it damages your puppy's teeth or gums. Chews such as antlers or bones are too hard for young teeth and should be reserved for older dogs (but keep in mind, they can damage adult enamel as well). On the other hand, you don't want to pick a chew that's too soft or easy to break pieces off of, like rawhide, as those pieces can cause indigestion, become choking hazards, or get lodged in the intestinal tract and require emergency surgery.

Bully sticks are a good option, but they can be rich and calorie-dense, so you don't want to give them to your puppy too often. C.E.T. Chews, made by Virbac, are beef-hide treats that help control tartar buildup on teeth, but they're generally devoured in a few minutes and don't offer substantial chewing time.

Chew treats should only be given when you can supervise your puppy. (Honestly, this goes for adult dogs, too.) Introduce them slowly and monitor for signs of digestive upset when feeding these. For longer-lasting chewing activities, you may want to consider chew toys or interactive feeding toys.

Human Food as Treats

Some dogs love human food, and there are several safe, low-calorie options you can employ as a tasty snack for your puppy. Plain rice cakes, diced carrots, green beans, and apples (with the core and seeds safely removed) are great crunchy treat options. Peanut butter is generally a dog favorite, but be mindful that it's high in fat, and always check the label for the sweetener xylitol, which is toxic to dogs. As detailed above, some human foods also make great high-value training treats.

CHAPTER 4

Exercise and Play

Play isn't just fun (and ador-able); it's also an essential part of a puppy's devel-opment and growth. During play, puppies are rehearsing important social and physical skills that will help them mature into well-adjusted adult dogs. This chapter will cover exercise, play, toys, and more.

Why Is Play Important?

Puppies love to play! Which is great because it helps them develop important skills. Play gives them the opportunity to explore canine social signals as they learn how to interpret body language from their playmates and practice how to respond to and navigate a large variety of interactions. Having abundant play opportunities as a puppy translates into having well-developed communication skills as an adult dog. Experience with different types of puppies and play styles will help your puppy gain confidence. Play also involves running, wrestling, wriggling, and twisting. These types of motor activity help develop healthy muscles, agility, and coordination as your puppy matures.

Remember that dogs explore the world with their mouths, and play is no exception. Play allows a puppy to practice using their mouth, and their playmate's response provides feedback on whether they were too rough. Over time, your puppy will learn to be aware of how much pressure it applies with its teeth. We call this "bite inhibition," and it's a skill best learned through play with littermates and other puppies. It's much trickier for human playmates to teach a puppy suitable bite pressure.

How Much Exercise Does a Puppy Need?

While there are no established guidelines for the exercise requirements of puppies, you can roughly gauge the amount based on your puppy's breed and age. Higher-energy dogs like border collies require more exercise than, say, laid-back Great Danes. As your puppy ages, they'll develop more stamina and a higher tolerance for physical exertion, so you can expect to see an increase in their exercise demands.

Choose from a variety of different activities, such as tug games, fetch, leash walks, and hide-and-seek to keep exercise fun for both you and your puppy. It's best to provide several short play opportunities throughout the day with plenty of time to rest in between. The Kennel Club recommends providing roughly five minutes of structured exercise per month of age, up to twice daily.

AGE	TOTAL EXERCISE PER DAY
8 weeks	10 minutes
12 weeks	15 minutes
16 weeks	20 minutes
20 weeks	25 minutes

Young dogs are still growing, and their growth plates remain "open" until roughly 9 to 10 months of age for smaller breeds and up to 18 months of age for larger breeds. Until then, your dog's joints are vulnerable, and excessive exercise can result in long-term damage. Help your puppy avoid actions like leaping over high objects, jumping down from heights, and repetitive exercise (such as jogging or biking) until they are older or your veterinarian gives you the green light. Larger-breed dogs may require exercise restrictions for longer, as their development takes more time to complete.

Unstructured exercise, such as play with toys, can be self-regulated by your puppy, so feel free to let this occur organically. You don't need to limit the amount of time your puppy plays around by themselves.

Toys

Puppies have their own tastes, so different puppies will prefer different types of toys. Provide your dog with a selection of toys and rotate them regularly to keep things novel and stimulating. No matter what type of toy your puppy likes playing with, it's always important to keep play safe. First, consider the toy's size and durability. A toy that's too small for your dog can become a choking hazard or cause serious health problems if swallowed. The same can happen if a piece of a toy comes off in your puppy's mouth during play, so regularly inspect your puppy's toys to ensure they're in good shape. Always supervise your puppy's toy time to make sure they don't chew off small pieces or otherwise run into trouble. (If your puppy is the kind who loves ripping pieces off toys and eating them, you should supervise toy time no matter how old they are.)

Let's take a look at some different types of toys, what they can do for your puppy, and how your puppy can enjoy them safely.

Chew Toys

Chewing is to a dog as getting into a good book or TV series is to a human: extremely satisfying and enriching. Chewing also exercises their jaws and stimulates their minds. For these reasons, it's important that your puppy have ample opportunity to chew, and chew toys provide an appropriate, "legal" outlet for them to do so without destroying your belongings. Not all dogs are the same, so your puppy may prefer softer rubber chew toys over harder plastic ones, or vice versa.

Kong-brand toys are popular and very durable, and Nyla-bone produces chew toys in a variety of textures and degrees of hardness.

It's safe to let your puppy chew while they still have puppy teeth, but you'll want to choose a teething toy until their adult teeth grow in. Similarly, bones and antlers are options for dogs who like harder textures—but not until they have mature teeth. Never give your dog cooked bones (like the bones left over after you eat chicken), as these can easily splinter and can be deadly if they damage the intestines. Inspect your puppy's chew toys regularly for any splinters or sharp edges and throw them away if you find any issues.

Teething Toys

Teething toys are a particular type of chew toy designed for puppies who are working on losing their baby teeth and getting their adult teeth. During this process, your puppy's gums will likely be sore and inflamed, much like a human baby's when their teeth first grow in. One of the best ways to soothe this discomfort is chewing, so it's important to supply your puppy with appropriate teething toys. You want a durable teething toy so your puppy can't chew off pieces and swallow them—but not so hard that it becomes a potential hazard to their teeth and gums. There are many toys on the market that are labeled specifically for puppy teething. Toys that are made to be frozen can also be soothing (but not ice cubes, which are hard enough to damage puppy teeth).

Squeaky Toys

Squeaky toys make a high-pitched squealing noise when your puppy bites down on them. These toys are very engaging and interactive for puppies, providing feedback when they bite hard

Tug-of-War: Rules of Engagement

I instruct clients to follow a set of three rules when playing tug-of-war to ensure the game is respectful and enjoyable for both parties.

1. **No teeth on skin.** If your puppy accidentally grabs your hand instead of the toy, say, "Ouch!" and immediately end the game by either removing or dropping the tug toy and walking away into a different room separated by a baby gate or door. You can either return to play after 5 to 10 minutes or end the game completely for now. The latter will provide a greater consequence for the puppy and teach them faster to be mindful of their mouth placement.

2. **Teach your dog a "Take it" cue and a "Drop it" cue.** Your puppy should only engage with tug toys when you give them permission to do so. "Take it" lets your puppy know that the game is on and they can grab the toy. "Drop it" communicates that your puppy needs to drop the toy now. Having clear cues and communication will prevent your puppy from lunging for toys in your hands and ensure that they listen to you throughout the game. (See chapter 8 to learn how to teach cues.)

3. **Take frequent breaks.** Throughout your tugging match, take short breaks, even for just a few seconds, in which you ask your dog to perform a calm, stationary behavior such as a "Sit" or a "Down." This prevents play from becoming too stimulating or out of control.

enough to elicit the squeak. The "squeak" is designed to emulate the sound of a prey animal, which in turn stimulates your dog's natural prey drive. The prey drive is a natural instinct in dogs, retained from their wolf ancestors, and it's important that we provide a legal and safe outlet for it. Squeaky toys can be an efficient way to meet this need, especially if you're playing with your puppy and making the toy "come to life." These toys let puppies practice "hunting": chasing, pouncing, biting, shaking, and maybe even shredding! Destroying toys is a normal and healthy behavior, but it's important to supervise your puppy with these toys so that if they do rip them open and pull out the stuffing or the treasured squeaker, you can confiscate these hazardous parts before they can ingest or choke on them.

Squeaky toys can become annoying to humans very quickly, so you may want to offer them in short sessions before swapping in a quieter toy option (see page 127 for information on performing a "bait and switch" to safely take away toys from your puppy).

Tug Toys

Tug toys are designed for your dog to grab hold of and pull on, while you or another dog hold on to the other end. The classic rope toy is one of the best tug toys around, but be careful that your dog doesn't start to chew strands off the rope. If the rope is starting to unravel, remove it from your puppy's toy rotation immediately, as strings can become dangerous foreign bodies if ingested. Other tug toys may have a bungee in them so there's more give and take in the toy during the game, making it very fun! Don't worry, tug-of-war won't teach your dog to be aggressive. In fact, it's a great healthy outlet for biting and mouthing behaviors.

Hard toys or toys with sharp protrusions aren't suitable for tugging, so if your puppy brings you a stick, it's best not to engage in a pulling match. Young puppies are still developing their jaw strength and gaining their adult teeth, so if you're playing tug-of-war, you should apply little, if any, pulling force. Rough games of tug-of-war can result in dental problems like crooked teeth (and can also cause damage in overly vigorous adult tuggers).

Fetch Toys

Fetch toys are designed for you to throw so that your puppy can chase and retrieve them. Toys like balls or Frisbees are the most common fetch toys, but really, any toy can be retrieved. Fetch is another great outlet for your dog's natural prey drive, so if your puppy enjoys "playing ball," give them lots of opportunities to do so. A company called Chuckit! sells particularly durable rubber balls along with a launcher that works kind of like a lacrosse stick, allowing you to throw the ball a great distance without working your shoulder too hard. These toys are great for dogs who really like fetch or who run very fast.

As always, consider the toy's size and durability so there's no danger of your dog choking on or swallowing an undersized ball. Inspect the area you're planning to play fetch in first so you know your dog won't fall in a ditch or find "snacks" you aren't aware of.

Plush Toys

Plush toys are soft and generally stuffed. If your puppy shreds a plush toy or pulls all the stuffing out, let them! They're rehearsing the "dissection" part of hunting. Just like it's important to give your dogs a legal outlet for their desire to chase moving things, it's important to give them an opportunity to dissect things. Take care to monitor your puppy, as a button nose can be quickly chewed off and swallowed, as can stuffing (which you may not even notice is missing). If you're hesitant to let your puppy shred pricey plush toys purchased from a store, look for cheap stuffed animals from yard sales or thrift stores. After washing them, let your puppy go to town ripping them to pieces.

Puzzle Toys

Your puppy needs to eat every day, so why not turn mealtime into a mentally stimulating activity as well? Dogs are natural scavengers, and by feeding our domesticated dogs from a food bowl, we effectively eliminate natural scavenging. You can change this by providing your dog with appropriate scavenging opportunities through puzzle toys and interactive feeding. These are designed to entertain, stimulate, and challenge your puppy by making them problem- solve to get their food.

A variety of puzzle toys exist on the

market, but some of the best toys can be made at home. The Internet is filled with ideas on how to make food puzzles for Fido out of everyday items. Some of my favorite toys include treat balls and classic Kongs, which have hollow middles you can stuff with dog-safe treats, such as plain yogurt, peanut butter (no xylitol!), applesauce, or even just regular kibble (I like to soak the kibble in water for a bit until it's mushy). To make a stuffed Kong more challenging and longer lasting, pop it in the freezer before feeding. All of these toys let your puppy invest time and energy into chewing, licking, and problem-solving to get the food out of the toy and into their belly.

Playmates

A puppy can have many different playmates, including you, your kids, and other animals. It's best to let your puppy play with people and dogs you know well initially, to help avoid stressful or negative outcomes.

Playing with Other Dogs

Playing with other dogs, particularly puppies, is a very important part of your puppy's development. Through play, your puppy will learn how to read body language, effectively communicate with their own body language, and inhibit their bite. Puppies are still developing their jaw strength, so it's quite safe for them to play and roughhouse with one another. When allowing your puppy to play with an adult dog, be aware of the size difference. A large adult dog might accidentally hurt your puppy with something as simple as a playful body check. Always supervise these play sessions and keep them short and sweet so that neither the puppy nor the adult dog becomes overwhelmed and both have the option to leave if they want to.

Here are some signs of good play.

Play bows. These are often used to initiate the start of play.

Role reversals. Your puppy and their playmate should switch roles regularly, from chaser to chased, or from top to bottom in a "wrestling" match.

Self-control and moderation. This means that any behavior such as biting or body slamming is delivered with reduced force. Your puppy is practicing gentler versions of classic fighting moves.

How to Perform a Consent Test

When two dogs are playing, it's meant to mimic the real thing (i.e., fighting or wrestling). Normal puppy play includes the flashing of teeth, snarling, growling, pinning each other, and play biting each other. If you're concerned a play session is getting too rough, perform a consent test to make sure both puppies still approve of what's going on.

1. Take hold of the puppy who appears to be playing too rough (the "bully puppy") by the collar or rear half of its body to stop the play momentarily. (It's important that you have first taught your puppy to love having their collar handled by pairing this action with tasty treats—see page 124.)

2. Restrain the rowdy pup briefly to see what the other puppy (the "victim puppy") chooses to do. Do they walk away or come charging back in for more?

3. If the victim puppy is eager to continue playing, you can let the play resume. If they run off, redirect the bully pup to a different playmate or activity.

Taking breaks. Short breaks (20 to 60 seconds) are important opportunities for the puppies to rest their bodies and settle themselves. Frequent breaks can keep the play from escalating and becoming too rough or intense.

Bouncy movement. Play should be goofy and clumsy. Bouncy movement and a loose body help dogs communicate to each other that this is all in good fun.

Playing with Human Adults

Playing with your puppy can be extremely rewarding for both of you, but you have to be smart about your puppy's biting habits. Avoid using your hands or feet as "toys" or ways of moving the puppy, as this can encourage them to nip and bite you. Instead, hold on to one of your puppy's toys and let your puppy play with it. This way, you're still interactive and engaged, but your puppy is not practicing using their teeth on your body.

Ensure that your puppy is respectful during play. Teeth should never contact human skin, and if they do, you should instantly stop the game. To do so, immediately remove the toy (or drop it if it's in your puppy's possession) and leave the room so that there's a gate or door between you and the puppy. The point of removing yourself is that you're also removing the puppy's opportunity for attention and interaction, which is a negative consequence. Wait 5 to 15 minutes before returning to the puppy. Incorporate frequent breaks into your play to prevent your puppy from getting overstimulated and playing too rambunctiously. Your puppy should never jump up to grab at toys in your hands, and instead should wait for a verbal cue to indicate it's okay to engage with the toy.

Playing with Kids

Dogs and younger kids should always be supervised when around one another, especially during play. This supervision has two main goals: to make sure your child isn't behaving inappropriately with your puppy, and to make sure your puppy isn't playing inappropriately with your child.

Appropriate behavior for kids means not using their hands or feet to engage with the puppy, as this will make them a prime target for play biting in the future. You also want to make sure your child is being respectful of your puppy—not pulling its tail, grabbing its ears, or sitting on it, even if your puppy doesn't "seem" to mind.

Appropriate behavior for puppies means no nipping, mouthing, or jumping up on the kids. Remember the "no teeth on human skin" rule! If the puppy is playing inappropriately, interrupt them immediately by performing a collar grab or gently restraining the puppy to prevent the play from continuing (as in a consent test). If the behavior continues, remove the puppy from the situation.

Fetch is a better game for kids to play with the puppy than tug-of-war, as it can be difficult for kids to implement tug rules, resulting in an overstimulated puppy. Dogs can be overwhelming for many kids, so make sure your child is enjoying the interaction, too!

Playing with Other Pets

When allowing your dog and cat to play, be aware of the size mismatch. A puppy is usually larger than a cat, making it easy for injury to occur, even unintentionally. Monitor play to ensure there are frequent breaks, that your puppy is reducing the force they use with the cat, and that the cat seems like an eager recipient of whatever your puppy is dishing out. It's a good idea to familiarize yourself with cat body language before allowing an interaction to occur. Make sure your cat has a clear exit and hiding places available should they get overwhelmed and wish to leave. Also, remember that cat claws can very easily cause serious damage. Cats retract their claws during normal play; end any play immediately if you notice your cat's claws are out.

If you own other pets like birds or rodents, it is safest not to allow play interactions with them and your puppy. The risk of injury with such small, delicate animals is too high.

Exercise by Breed

Some breeds require specific exercise considerations. Brachycephalic (flat-faced) dogs like pugs and bulldogs can't breathe or pant very effectively, so they may get winded much faster and struggle to cool themselves off for longer than other breeds. Long, hard periods of exercise in high temperatures can be very dangerous for these dogs. Conversely, some breeds of dogs require significantly more exercise than others, particularly the "working breed" category of dogs, which includes Weimaraners, retrievers, shepherds, collies, hounds, and huskies. Other breeds, like Great Danes, have

The Zoomies

"The zoomies" is a common name for what are technically called frenetic random activity periods, or FRAPs. If you've observed them, you know they're exactly what they sound like! Your dog will zoom around, running back and forth or spinning around repetitively. These episodes are thought to be a way of releasing excess energy in one big burst. Luckily, zoomies are usually brief. There may be certain times of day when your puppy tends to experience them. If your puppy is predictable, you can usher them outside during these times to give them more space to run and keep your belongings safe from the chaos. Your puppy may continue this behavior as an adult, but it will likely be less frequent and shorter in duration. If you notice your puppy is experiencing the zoomies several times a day, they may be lacking an outlet for their energy, so consider increasing their daily exercise.

significantly lower exercise requirements and do better with shorter outings, especially when they're older.

As always, every dog is an individual, and your puppy may not exhibit the "typical" traits for their breed. What's most important is supervising their exercise and paying attention to signs that they're either tired or ready for more.

Nap Time

Young puppies require 18 to 20 hours of sleep a day, as opposed to adult dogs' 12 to 14 hours (some larger breeds of dogs, like mastiffs and St. Bernards, sleep even more). Ample sleep is important for healthy growth and development, and it allows puppies to process all the things they've experienced while awake. Puppy naps can last 30 minutes to 2 hours and may come upon the puppy very quickly. One minute, the puppy is teaching their ball a lesson, and the next moment, they're sleeping in a heap on the floor. Let them rest!

It's helpful to have a crate or other safe napping place where the puppy can sleep undisturbed. Encourage your puppy into their crate when they show signs of sleepiness and reward them for using the crate on their own. Puppies, much like young children, don't always know when or how to wind down when they're feeling tired, so settle your puppy in for a nap proactively when you see signs of overtired behavior, such as rough play, pestering, harder biting, frustration, or "the zoomies." Establishing a bedtime routine will help create a sleep schedule for your puppy. For a consistent bedtime, do your last walk of the day and final potty break at roughly the same time every evening, then settle your puppy in their crate or bed.

Where Can My Puppy Exercise?

No matter your lifestyle or where you live, you can find a place for your puppy to get the right amount of play and exercise. Though the risk for exposure to disease increases significantly in certain public places like dog parks and pet stores, your puppy doesn't have to stay completely indoors until they're fully vaccinated. Ask your vet for guidance on low-risk areas like backyards and reputable puppy classes.

In the Yard

If you have a yard, it's usually the best place for your puppy to play, as you'll have ample room for activities like fetch, tug-of-war, and hide-and-seek. Hide-and-seek can be a physically and mentally stimulating game, as your puppy is moving while also using their problem-solving skills and their nose to find the hidden food, toys, or person.

Your backyard is also a great place to host puppy playdates with other dogs. Of course, you'll want to make sure that any dog your puppy is in contact with is fully vaccinated and not showing any signs of illness, such as coughing, sneezing, vomiting, or diarrhea. You'll also want to make sure the dogs are taking frequent play breaks, play remains consensual for both animals (see page 64 for more on consent tests), and you have plenty of fresh water available for them to cool off.

Indoors

Playing indoors can be fun for your puppy, especially if the weather outside is cold or wet. Mental games can challenge your puppy's brain more than their body, but they can be equally exhausting—if not more so. Scent-work games (sniffing out hidden food or toys), puzzle toys, or basic training sessions can be great for preventing boredom and tiring out a dog indoors.

Make these games fun and novel. Teach a new trick instead of working on "Stay," change the room in which you hide your dog's toy, or hide multiple toys and treats to make the search even more exhilarating! Interactive games, like tug-of-war, hide-and-seek, and fetch (if you have the space for it), can be fun for both you and your puppy.

On a Leash

Walks are a great way for your puppy to explore the world while also getting some structured exercise, but discuss with your vet any disease-prevention measures you should be taking, and avoid jogging or running until your puppy's growth plates are completely closed (around 9 to 18 months of age). If your puppy is not fully vaccinated, avoid areas heavily populated with dogs, such as dog parks or popular walking trails.

Once your puppy is fully vaccinated, you'll have more freedom. Take a different route often when you walk your puppy; even a couple of blocks can increase the novelty and excitement of the walk. Allow your puppy to explore and take frequent sniff breaks along the way. This is a fantastic form of mental stimulation, as dogs gather most of their information about the environment through their nose. Using a "Let's go" cue and rewarding with a treat when you want your puppy to stop sniffing is a great way to control the pace of your walk while still letting your puppy enjoy their surroundings. (See page 160 for more on leash training.)

Out in the World

Once your puppy is fully vaccinated, there are many outdoor adventures awaiting you—hiking, swimming, dog parks (see page 135), and the beach, to name a few. Be smart when you head out to explore with your puppy. Know the rules of the area you're going to. Is it off-leash or on-leash only? How long is the hike, and how rough is the terrain? Will your puppy have to walk on rocks or pavement that are in direct sunlight? (Your dog's paws can be injured by exposure to the elements, walking in the snow, or walking during peak sun hours. If the pavement is hot to your foot, it's hot to your dog's!)

Once you're there, pay attention. Is your dog enjoying the activity, or are they overwhelmed and frightened? Make sure you're okay leaving whatever you had planned if it's too much for your puppy, whether it's playing with other dogs at the dog park or attending a friend's backyard barbecue. If you're planning off-leash activities, ensure that your puppy has been trained in reliable recall and is wearing a secure collar with ID on it, in case you become separated. To prevent heat stroke or dehydration, pack a collapsible travel bowl and enough water for you *and* your puppy.

CHAPTER 5

Grooming

Grooming is not just an important part of keeping your puppy fun to snuggle and looking cute—it's also important for their overall health and a great way to build trust with body handling. This section will cover basic grooming recommendations to keep your puppy's skin, coat, teeth, and nails in tip-top shape.

Skin and Coat

Your puppy's coat is what most people associate with "grooming"—but there's much more to it than that. This section will cover the considerations you need to take when caring for the health, integrity, and appearance of your puppy's coat and skin.

Types of Coat

Did you know that though most dogs have fur, some have hair? Hair, which is more like the hair humans have, has a longer growing cycle, meaning it sheds less frequently. It's also smoother and finer to the touch, but it traps dirt more easily (partly due to the less frequent shedding), which can easily result in tangles and mats. Dogs with continuously growing hair (such as shih tzus or Yorkshire terriers) and curly-coated breeds (such as poodles and Portuguese water dogs) require regular trimming by a groomer to keep their coats at a manageable and healthy length. They may also need their faces trimmed now and then to prevent their hair from getting in their eyes and obscuring their vision.

Dogs with a "double coat," like huskies and Bernese mountain dogs, have not one but two layers of fur: an undercoat and a topcoat. The topcoat acts as a guard, repelling water, and the undercoat serves as an insulating layer. People sometimes mistakenly believe they should shave double-coated dogs to prevent mats or keep them cool in hot weather. Never do this! Shaving a double-coated dog does not help keep them cool; it just damages the topcoat. The way to maintain a healthy, clean double coat is to regularly brush it, trimming only the long hairs by the legs, bums, tails, and feet, if needed.

Brushing and Combing

Brushing your puppy has numerous benefits, including removing tangles, dead hair, and dead skin cells; stimulating the skin's surface; and distributing natural skin oils. Brushing can even be relaxing for some dogs, much like a massage, and can be a great bonding experience for you and your puppy. Remember to make your puppy's first encounters with brushing positive by using treats! One brush stroke equals one treat. Gradually increase the number of brush strokes before you feed a treat as your puppy accepts the handling.

How often you brush your puppy will really depend on its coat type. Short-haired breeds, such as Dobermans and dalmatians, do fine with once-weekly brushing, whereas long-coated breeds, like retrievers and spaniels, benefit from daily grooming to maintain tangle-free tresses. Leaving your dog's coat unbrushed for too long can result in painfully tight mats that may require shaving, professional grooming, or even grooming under sedation. Regular maintenance is key!

There are multiple types of brushes available for dog grooming, and much like the frequency of brushing, the type you select will depend largely on your puppy's coat. A brush might be designed to remove mats or tangles, clear out loose fur from the undercoat, or maintain the topcoat. At the store, ask for help selecting a brush if you're not sure you have the right type, or book an appointment with a professional groomer to learn some more tips specific to your dog's needs.

Here are some of the most common types of brushes available.

Bristle brushes are the most versatile. Pick a brush with shorter, denser bristles for short-coated dogs and longer, more spaced-out bristles for long-coated dogs. These brushes remove dirt and loose hair and stimulate the skin.

Slicker brushes are designed to remove loose hair and dirt but will also remove tangles and some mats from short- to medium-length coats. Don't apply too much pressure, as the teeth could become uncomfortable.

Undercoat rakes and other "deshedding" tools (like the Furminator) are designed to remove loose fur from the undercoat without damaging the healthy topcoat. Breeds like German shepherds and huskies benefit greatly from these types of brushes, especially during spring and fall, when their coat is transitioning with the seasons. Make sure the length of the "pins" or teeth matches the length of your dog's fur—too short and you'll miss the inner layers of the undercoat, too long and you may irritate the skin.

To Pay or Not to Pay?

When does your puppy need to see a groomer? That depends on a few factors. How dirty is your dog? How capable are you of tackling the job? What type of coat does your puppy have, and does it need trimming? Groomers are professionals at tackling a dirty and disheveled dog coat. They have the proper tools on hand and are much more efficient at the job than you or I. Groomers don't just rid your dog's coat of dirt, debris, and tangles; they also thoroughly brush out any dead or loose hair, trim hair where required, and may clean your dog's ears and clip their nails. Long- or curly-coated breeds need to see a groomer more regularly, whereas some short-coated dogs may never need to see one at all, depending on your ability to maintain their skin and coat at home.

If your puppy will be making frequent groomer visits, introduce them to the experience in a positive way early on. Take several "fun trips" to the groomer—just go in and receive treats, with no actual grooming. A Fear Free Certified groomer will be patient and gentle-handed, and will ensure the first groom is a positive experience by only doing as much handling as your puppy will happily tolerate. Ask to stay and watch the appointment so you can pick up tips. You can also ask for homework to help your dog learn the necessary handling and get used to the different tools.

Bathing

How often should you give your puppy a bath? It really depends. If your dog starts to develop an odor, a bath is a good idea. A roll in a fresh mud puddle (or something worse)? Bath time! Most dogs do fine with baths a few times a year at most, and this is usually more for odor control than for coat or skin health. If your dog has a medical skin condition, your veterinarian may recommend frequent baths to help treat or manage this—but bathing your puppy too often can actually *cause* skin irritation by stripping the natural, healthy oils from their coat, so don't do this unless your vet specifically recommends it.

When bathing your puppy, use shampoos specifically formulated for dogs; human shampoos can irritate your dog's skin. Leftover shampoo can cause irritation, too, so rinse it out well. When you think you've rinsed enough, rinse once more to be sure!

How to Bathe Your Puppy

Introduce bathing to your puppy early on. As with any novel and potentially scary experience, it's important to make the experience positive and not overwhelming. You can do this by (a) breaking the process down into small, achievable steps, and (b) pairing baths with treats.

Start by bringing your puppy into the bathroom and feeding them 5 to 10 treats in a row before letting them leave the room. Do this multiple times, until your puppy is comfortable and confident in the space. Next, feed your puppy treats in the empty bathtub! (You can either lift them into the tub or encourage them to jump in themselves, whatever they're most comfortable with. Make sure you have a nonslip mat on the bottom of your tub so your puppy doesn't get scared or hurt.) Next, feed your puppy treats in a bathtub pre-filled with one inch of water. Gradually fill the tub up more each session and experiment with gently splashing your puppy. Slosh water up one leg, followed immediately by praise and treats. Only increase the amount of splashing and handling as your puppy is confident and comfortable.

Teeth

Puppies require oral maintenance. Brushing their teeth daily is the best way to manage plaque and tartar buildup, just like in humans. Once-a-week brushing is not as ideal, but it's still far superior to no brushing at all, so do what you can to give your puppy's teeth adequate attention. Use a toothpaste created for dogs, as human toothpastes may contain ingredients that are toxic to dogs. Dog toothpaste also comes in flavors that appeal to them more, such as chicken and beef. Toothbrushes designed for dogs are easier to use than human toothbrushes, with smaller heads that fit their mouths. You can also purchase a rubber finger toothbrush that you put on like a finger puppet for ease of use.

There are many dental chews and treats on the market. Some use the act of chewing to help scrape plaque off teeth and stimulate healthy gums, while others are formulated with specific ingredients like enzymes that contribute to overall oral health. If you don't brush your puppy's teeth, these treats are better than nothing. Be mindful of the extra calories and feed them in moderation.

Your puppy's teeth should be examined for dental disease at every veterinary appointment. Smaller dogs are more prone to dental disease and generally need cleanings earlier and more frequently. Breeds like Chihuahuas commonly retain their baby teeth even after their adult teeth have come in, which can cause crowding and make it easier for plaque to build up. These teeth sometimes need to be extracted if they don't fall out on their own. Note that while your puppy is transitioning from baby to adult teeth, they lose their teeth just like humans do, so don't be alarmed if you find a bloody

Say No to Anesthetic-Free Dental Cleanings!

Anesthetic-free dental cleanings are performed without the use of anesthetic drugs while your dog is awake, generally by groomers. This is a bad idea for a multitude of reasons. Most dogs don't enjoy having their mouths handled or teeth cleaned (most humans don't like going to the dentist either!), so they usually need to be restrained to some degree during the procedure, which can be scary and stressful for them. Even with restraint, any sudden movements, even slight ones, can result in injury to your dog's mouth. On top of that, the person performing the cleaning can only assess the health of the tooth surface *above* the gumline. They can't clean below the gumline, where most dental disease originates. These cleanings may make your puppy's teeth look whiter, but white teeth don't necessarily translate into a clean and healthy mouth. If you think your dog's teeth need cleaning past the brushing you can do at home, consult your vet about performing a thorough and safe dental cleaning under anesthesia.

molar on the floor or blood on your puppy's chew toys during this time.

How to Brush Your Dog's Teeth

Much like bathing, you want to introduce toothbrushing to your dog early on, in a slow and positive way, repeating each step several times, until your dog is clearly comfortable and not avoiding the contact. Start by introducing your puppy to the toothbrush (without toothpaste), then touch the toothbrush to your puppy's cheek for five seconds. Next, show your puppy the toothbrush with toothpaste on it, which they can lick off if they want. Feed them a few treats at each step.

To get your puppy used to having their mouth handled, start by simply touching their muzzle for one second, feeding them a treat, and taking your hand away. Gradually increase how long you leave your hand on the muzzle, then cup your hand over the top of the muzzle, put gentle pressure on the muzzle, and so on, eventually opening the top of the mouth to expose the teeth. Again, feed a few treats at each step.

Now to start brushing! Start with one to two seconds of gentle brushing (followed by a treat, of course), and gradually increase the duration of brushing and the pressure applied.

Nails

Regular nail trimming is important in order to keep your puppy's nails at a safe and healthy length. When they get too long, they reduce your dog's traction and cause abnormal paw placement when walking, which can result in strain on the supporting structures in the leg over time. Plus, long nails are at a higher risk of breaking, which can be painful.

I recommend weekly nail trims, which not only maintain a healthy nail length but also make the job a lot faster and easier to perform. Why? In the core of a dog's nail is something called the "quick," which supplies blood and nerves to the nail. Humans have it under our nails too—hence, the phrase "cut me to the quick." Just like with humans, a normal nail trim is painless. But if your puppy is crying, you might have cut their nails too short and hit the quick, which can be very painful (think of how much it hurts when your finger-nail gets injured!) and can result in bleeding. Having styptic powder on hand will help stop the bleeding and reduce the pain if you do accidentally clip the quick. Place some styp-tic powder in the palm of your hand and gently press the bleeding nail into the powder for a minute or two to stop the bleeding.

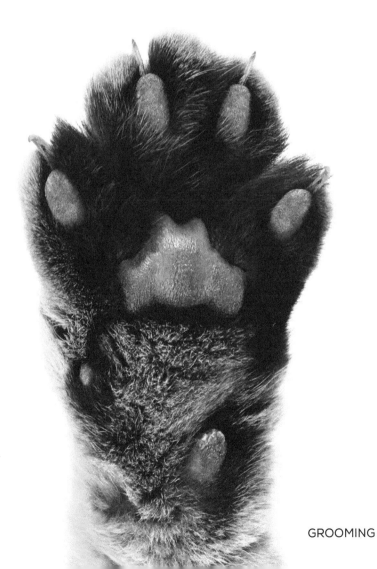

There are many different nail trimming devices for dogs on the market. Nail clipper styles are a personal preference, so test them out in your hand before you purchase anything. Scissor clippers are good for bigger, thicker nails. Guillotine clippers work just as their name implies, with a wide blade that slides down through a set of grooves. A motorized Dremel nail grinder files down nails instead of clipping them, but be aware that the whirring noise might spook your puppy initially and long toe hairs can get caught in the machinery.

How to Clip Your Dog's Nails

Nail trims can be traumatic for many dogs, and some even need to be sedated for the procedure at a vet clinic. That's why early exposure and handling of the feet from a young age is so crucial. As with any new form of handling, start early and introduce nail clipping with patience and positivity. Reward your puppy with praise and treats for sniffing the clippers, then work up to touching the clippers to their body, starting with the shoulder and gradually working your way toward the upper leg, ankle, and eventually the paw. Expose your puppy to paw handling by first simply touching the paw, then gently holding it, then grasping it more firmly, feeding them treats all the while. Now incorporate the clippers. Start

Frito Paws

Have you ever noticed your puppy's paws smelling an awful lot like corn chips? Your puppy's paws may develop an odor nicknamed "Frito paws" or "Frito feet," which is the result of bacteria they pick up from everyday dirt and debris coupled with the saliva from when they clean their paws. If you notice your puppy's feet are stinky, try washing them in warm water with a mild, hypoallergenic soap. Make sure to rinse and dry the paws well, or the bacteria will just multiply. Trimming any long hairs between the toes and drying the paws after walks outside can help prevent bacterial growth from recurring. If your puppy's paws have redness, swelling, or discharge, that's more serious than Frito paws, and it's time for a vet trip.

by holding the paw and touching the clippers to the nail, and work up to taking a snip! One nail equals one treat at the beginning. Keep your expectations realistic. Your puppy may only be comfortable having a few nails clipped, so be prepared to stop and try again the next day.

If you've never clipped a dog's nails before, I recommend getting a quick lesson from your puppy's groomer or veterinary team. They can show you how to evaluate the length of your puppy's quick and the appropriate angle at which to cut the nail.

Eyes and Ears

Puppies' eyes and ears generally don't require frequent cleaning or grooming, but there are a few exceptions. As previously mentioned, some dogs require trimming to keep the hair on their face out of their eyes. Some white-colored dogs are also prone to pinkish or reddish-brown "tear stains" under their eyes, which are caused by porphyrins, a natural component of canine tears and saliva. To avoid staining, wipe under your puppy's eyes twice daily with a warm cloth to dilute and wash away the tears, starting close to the eye and moving outward. If you're worried your dog produces an excessive amount of tears, visit the vet to ensure there is no health condition that needs attention.

Compared to dogs with upright ears, dogs with droopy ears naturally have less airflow and more heat and moisture in their ears. This can become a breeding ground for bacteria, so check them regularly for redness, discharge, or an off-putting odor. If you're concerned about the amount of hair in your dog's ear canal, speak to your vet or groomer about trimming it to allow for more adequate circulation. If your dog is prone to ear debris or infections, your vet may prescribe regular cleaning using a safe over-the-counter or prescription ear-cleaning solution.

CHAPTER 6

Raising a Healthy Puppy

P uppyhood involves frequent veterinary visits, whether for routine preventive reasons or when dealing with injury or sickness. This chapter will guide you on how to keep your puppy healthy, how to care for them when they get sick, and when to get the professionals involved.

Visiting the Vet

Your puppy will likely make their debut trip to the veterinary clinic between six and eight weeks of age, which is probably before you even bring them home. Your vet will perform a full physical examination, checking your puppy from nose to tail. Assuming they're healthy, your puppy will then receive their first vaccinations and be dewormed. They will continue to visit the vet approximately once a month until 16 weeks of age so the vet can monitor their growth, give them booster shots, and provide repeat deworming. These visits are important to ensure a healthy and disease-free puppy.

The vet can be a very overwhelming place for a young puppy. There are lots of new smells, sounds, and sights—and not many dogs enjoy needles. Search for a Fear Free Certified clinic and help your puppy enjoy the vet by making frequent "fun trips" to the clinic. Go armed with your puppy's favorite snacks solely for the purpose of meeting the staff, eating treats, exploring the clinic, eating treats, and maybe touring the exam room (don't forget the treats!). During your puppy's vaccinations, a steady flow of treats or even canned dog food smeared on the exam table can prove to be a trusty distraction.

Vaccinations

Some of the first medical attention a puppy receives is a schedule of routine vaccinations. Vaccinations are important to protect your puppy from dangerous, potentially fatal diseases. Vaccinations can be split into two categories: (1) core vaccines, which vets recommend all dogs have, and (2) lifestyle vaccines, which might be recommended if your puppy does lots of traveling, commonly visits heavily populated dog venues, or gets a lot

Pet Insurance

Much like health insurance, pet insurance can help offset routine and emergency medical expenses. Many pet-insurance plans are starting to incorporate coverage for routine health care, such as vaccinations, annual physical exams, and dental care. Some plans might even cover training costs, so ask your provider. If you decide to purchase pet insurance for your puppy, it's best to do it right away, as most companies won't cover preexisting conditions. This is especially important for breeds with known health conditions (see page 111 for some of the most common). If you choose not to purchase pet insurance, it's a good idea to set up an emergency pet fund for emergencies or surprise vet costs.

of exposure to wildlife or water sources. Your vet team will ask you questions to determine the best vaccination protocol for your puppy.

The core vaccinations are the combo DAPP (distemper, adenovirus, parvovirus, and sometimes parainfluenza) and rabies vaccines. Although rabies is not present in all areas, it's still considered a core vaccination due to its 100 percent fatality rate and risk of transfer to people.

Lifestyle vaccines are Bordetella (kennel cough), leptospirosis, and canine Lyme disease. Whether your vet will recommend these vaccinations depends on your puppy's lifestyle and travel history, as well as the prevalence of these diseases in your region.

The cost of vaccinations depends on your state or province. The average vaccine appointment, which also includes

VACCINE	AGE OF INITIAL ADMINISTRATION	BOOSTER SCHEDULE
DAPP	6 to 8 weeks	Every 2 to 4 weeks until the puppy is 16 weeks of age, 1-year booster, and then every 1 to 3 years thereafter
Leptospirosis	8 to 9 weeks	Booster 2 to 4 weeks after initial vaccination, then annually thereafter
Canine Lyme Disease	8 to 9 weeks	Booster 2 to 4 weeks after initial vaccination, then annually thereafter
Bordetella (Kennel Cough)	8 to 16 weeks	May require a booster 2 to 4 weeks after initial vaccination, depending on which formulation is used, and then annually as recommended
Rabies	12 to 16 weeks	1-year booster, then every 1 to 3 years thereafter

SOURCE: AMERICAN ANIMAL HOSPITAL ASSOCIATION

a physical examination, can range from about $70 to $120. Additional lifestyle vaccinations will usually cost $20 to $30 per vaccine. Animal shelters may offer cheaper options.

Microchipping

A microchip is an electronic device, about the size of a grain of rice, that is injected under your puppy's skin. When a microchip scanner passes over it, radio waves activate the chip and display the associated numbers. Microchipping is a worldwide identification system, so no matter where your dog is, the chip can be scanned. A microchip can be placed at any time with a needle only slightly larger than the one used for your puppy's routine vaccinations, no sedation or anesthetic required. It's common for a vet to implant one during your puppy's spay or neuter procedure. Another permanent ID option is a tattoo, generally placed in your pet's ear. Tattoos can be read by anybody—no scanner necessary—but they can also fade and become illegible over time. Either way, the ID you choose is only as good as the information it provides, so keep your phone number and address up to date.

Getting Your Puppy Fixed

Getting your puppy "fixed" means surgically removing their reproductive organs. Spaying is the procedure for female dogs and involves the removal of the ovaries and potentially the uterus. Neutering is the procedure for male dogs and involves removing the testicles. Neutering is a less invasive procedure, as you don't have to open the abdominal wall to perform the surgery (unless your puppy has a condition called "cryptorchidism," which means that one or both testicles haven't descended from the abdomen into the scrotum).

Fixing your pet is recommended to prevent unwanted litters, unplanned breeding, and certain health and behavioral concerns. Unspayed female dogs (also referred to as "unaltered" or "intact") are at risk of uterine infections and mammary tumors. Unaltered males are at an increased risk of prostate and testicular cancer. Fixing your dog may also help control behavioral concerns, such as roaming, mounting, and urine marking. The most common recommendation is to wait to spay or neuter until after six months of age, but you should discuss this issue with your vet, as it may vary by breed.

Common Parasites

Parasites and pets are no strangers to one another, but luckily, there are tried-and-true ways of preventing your puppy from becoming inhabited by creepy crawlies and treating them if they do show up. This section will cover common canine parasites and what you need to do about them.

Roundworms

Roundworms are one of the most common intestinal parasites. According to the CDC, "almost all puppies are born already infected," so routine deworming is important. Your puppy might also acquire roundworms by ingesting infected soil, feces, birds, or rodents. While these parasites can fly under the radar in small numbers, in large numbers, they can cause intestinal blockage and even death. They can also travel to the lungs and cause pneumonia. A puppy with roundworms might exhibit a "potbellied" appearance, scooting behavior, and/or weight loss. You may find visible worms in the puppy's stool or vomit. If you suspect your puppy has intestinal worms, contact your vet immediately. They'll likely ask you to bring in a stool sample for testing. A puppy's routine deworming schedule may increase in frequency if there is an active infestation.

Roundworms can be passed along to humans, so this is another important reminder to wash your hands, routinely pick up your dog's poop, and avoid letting your puppy lick your face. Hygiene is particularly important for young kids, who tend to put everything in their mouths.

Heartworms

Transmitted by infected mosquitoes, heartworms live in the heart, lungs, and associated blood vessels. There are few to no early symptoms of heartworm, but the longer the infection persists and the heavier the worm load, the more you may start to see a mild but persistent cough, reluctance to exercise, post-activity fatigue, decreased appetite, and weight loss. Heart disease may be coupled with a swollen belly from fluid accumulation. Over time, these worms can cause severe lung disease, heart failure, and organ damage.

It's important to know the risk of heartworm in your area or the areas you're traveling to. If there is a known risk, check with your vet about using a monthly heartworm preventive. Depending on your puppy's age, the vet might want to test for heartworms first, as starting preventive care with an existing infection can be dangerous. However, even though a puppy can't be tested for heartworm until seven months of age, you can use preventive medication against heartworms as early as eight weeks.

Fleas

Fleas are external parasites that bite your dog (and, potentially, you), sucking their blood as food. They're usually spread via contact with a dog, home, or area that has fleas. They can jump a remarkable distance, which allows them to easily

travel from host to host. Signs that your dog has fleas include itchiness and scratching/chewing, small red bumps on the skin, and small dark specks (flea poop) throughout their coat. You might also spot the dark brown bugs themselves as they scurry through your dog's fur, particularly at the base of the tail, the neck, the groin, and the back of the hind legs. Some dogs may develop a condition called flea allergy dermatitis in which the skin around flea bites becomes red, irritated, and sometimes infected. Puppies with a heavy flea burden can develop anemia, which can be life-threatening if left untreated.

If your puppy has fleas, they're also at risk of contracting a tapeworm if they ingest a tapeworm-contaminated flea when grooming themselves. Tapeworms, like roundworms, can cause weight loss and scooting and are often diag-nosed by finding physical evidence in the dog's stool or vomit. People also report finding what look like sesame seeds or rice granules in their pet's bedding; these are dried tapeworm segments, and they indicate your puppy should be on flea prevention, even if you haven't seen any fleas.

Fleas are a bigger problem when the weather is warm. Freezing temperatures may kill fleas or cause them to lie dormant until warmer weather wakes them back up. If you live in a region that doesn't get consistent freezing temperatures in the winter, you'll need to treat your dog for fleas year-round. The best way to prevent fleas is to treat your dog with a topical or oral prescription product that kills fleas on contact. Not all flea prevention products are created equal, and in fact, some can be harmful to your puppy, so speak with your vet about which products are safest and most effective.

Ticks

Ticks are another external bloodsucking parasite. They latch on to your dog (or you) to ingest blood, and then, once they're full, detach and fall off. Ticks can be very difficult to remove; if it's done incorrectly, the head and mouthpiece could be left in the dog's skin, which can cause serious health concerns. Ticks are carriers of several potentially life-threatening diseases, such as Rocky Mountain spotted fever, Lyme disease, and tick paralysis, a serious condition in which a dog's whole

Flea

Tick

body becomes increasingly paralyzed due to a neurotoxin in the tick's saliva. A dog who has been bitten by a tick might scratch or bite at the region but may not show symptoms of a tick-borne illness for weeks or months.

As with fleas, the best prevention against ticks is a monthly oral or topical treatment. Some products on the market work against fleas and ticks, as well as some internal parasites. Speak with your vet about the prevalence of tick-borne illnesses in your area and which form of tick prevention is right for you and your puppy.

Medication

Some common medications that your puppy may need at some point include antibiotics, nonsteroidal anti-inflammatories, antiparasitics, and antihistamines. Many dogs will happily take a pill if it's wrapped in a piece of cheese or lunch meat, but always check with your vet first to ensure that it's okay for your puppy to take their medication with food. Sometimes tossing the treat for the dog to catch can prevent them from chewing too much and deciphering the foreign pill in the middle of their tasty snack. There are even treats called Pill Pockets specifically designed to aid with pill delivery. If your dog won't voluntarily eat their pill, ask your vet team to demonstrate how to pill your puppy—that is, how to physically place the pill in the back of their mouth so they swallow it. This can be easy to accomplish if you know what to do and how to do it carefully.

Some medications come in a liquid form. You can drizzle these over some canned food, but you must ensure that the dog eats the entire meal and no medication is left on the sides of the dish. You can also syringe small portions of the medication into the dog's cheek pouch, ensuring that you pause between tastes to allow the dog to lick and swallow the medication rather than spitting it out. (Chase it with small, frequent syringefuls of low-sodium beef or chicken broth to offset the taste of the medication and help your dog enjoy this type of handling.) Make sure you always follow the medication with a tasty treat.

Ear and eye medications can cause more of a fight, as they require more handling to safely administer. Teaching your puppy to be comfortable with having their eyes and ears handled from a young age can aid you in future medicating. Always reward every handling moment with a high-value treat and provide a massive jackpot (multiple treats and celebration) after the medication has been applied. Regular maintenance handling in between actual medication administrations can help maintain positive associations with this type of handling. Your puppy will also learn that 99 percent of the time, this handling simply results in treats, so the 1 percent where something funny actually happens (like ear solution being squirted into their ear) is not such a big deal.

Note: Never give any human medications to your puppy unless you have been specifically instructed to do so by your vet!

When Your Puppy Eats Something They Shouldn't

Puppies explore the world with their mouths, which often results in biting, chewing, and potentially swallowing things that shouldn't be consumed. This section covers what to do if your puppy has eaten something that's not good for them and how to handle these situations if they arise.

Poisoning

If your puppy accidentally ingests a toxic substance, call your vet or poison control immediately. The Pet Poison Helpline (855-764-7661) is staffed with experts who can help you determine what you should be watching for and how you should proceed following an ingestion. Never try to induce vomiting in your puppy unless instructed to do so by a professional; vomiting up certain substances can cause serious issues. Signs and symptoms of poisoning will vary greatly depending on what your puppy has eaten.

Choking

Some items, if swallowed, can become lodged in your puppy's mouth or throat. This is a life-threatening situation, as a foreign object can obstruct the airway and prevent your puppy from breathing. Signs that your puppy might be choking include pawing at their mouth, gagging or gasping, not responding, or losing consciousness. If your puppy can't breathe, use both hands to open their mouth, one hand on the upper jaw and one on the lower. (Be cautious of the potential bite risk when doing this; panicked animals are not generally mindful of human fingers.) If you can see and easily hook the obstruction with your finger, you should do so, but if it's too deep and you must reach or dig for it, stop and transport your puppy to the vet immediately. Attempting to reach a deeply lodged obstruction can push it deeper and cause damage to the surrounding tissues.

Swallowing Foreign Objects

Swallowing foreign objects is a common concern with puppies. Dogs don't readily know what's edible and what's not, and their standards of what may make a tasty snack differ greatly from ours. Foreign bodies can be a medical emergency if swallowed and should not be taken lightly. If a foreign object is tightly obstructed, it can quickly cause damage to the surrounding tissues, potentially resulting in death.

If your dog has just ingested a foreign item, call your vet to see if they recommend inducing vomiting. Depending on the size, texture, and material, some objects (such as baby

Poisonous to Puppies

Here are some common household items that are poisonous to puppies (and adult dogs as well). This list is not exhaustive, so if you're ever unsure, contact your vet or poison control immediately.

FOOD

- Alcohol
- Apricot (pit, leaves, and stem)
- Bread dough, unbaked
- Caffeine
- Cherries
- Chocolate
- Garlic
- Grapes/raisins
- Macadamia nuts
- Mushrooms (some varieties)
- Onions
- Salt
- Xylitol (artificial sweetener)

MEDICATIONS

- Acetaminophen (Tylenol)
- Antidepressants
- Marijuana and other drugs
- Stimulants

PLANTS

- Autumn crocus
- Azalea
- Cyclamen
- Daffodils
- Dieffenbachia
- Hyacinths
- Lilies (not all varieties)
- Lily of the valley
- Oleander
- Sago palm
- Tulips

CHEMICALS

- Antifreeze
- Blue-green algae
- Compost bins/piles
- Herbicides
- Mole/gopher bait
- Mothballs
- Rodenticides (e.g., rat poison)
- Slug/snail bait

socks) can be thrown up safely, whereas others can cause significant damage. Some smaller items might be able to pass through your dog's system with no issue. Signs that your puppy may have ingested a foreign item include vomiting, diarrhea or constipation, lack of appetite, lethargy, and depression. Your vet can take an X-ray of your dog's intestinal tract to search for the foreign item. Depending on its place in your dog's digestive system, the vet may recommend removing it surgically or endoscopically.

Common Health Problems

Just like us, puppies get sick from time to time. Knowing about common health concerns in advance can make these situations less stressful when they arise. This section will go over common health problems—what they are, how to identify them, and what to do about them.

Dermatitis (Skin Irritation)

Skin irritation is generally caused by hypersensitivity to a substance—such as plant pollens, dust mites, molds, or, less frequently, foods—in the puppy's environment. It can also be a hereditary condition. Signs include scratching, licking, chewing, and rubbing affected areas, particularly the paws, face, and rear end. When the dog chews at the area trying to relieve its discomfort, it can lead to hair loss, reddening and thickening of the skin, and secondary infections.

Your puppy's vet will likely first rule out any fungal, yeast, and bacterial infections, as well as external parasites, such as fleas, ticks, and lice. Avoiding known allergens will help manage reactions, but when you're unable to do so, your puppy may be prescribed medications such as antihistamines or steroids to control the reactions, as well as antibiotics if a secondary infection has developed.

First-Aid Kit

When you become a puppy owner, it's important to have a small first-aid kit on hand in the event of an emergency or injury. Keep your supplies in a labeled box with a tight-fitting lid in an easily accessible area of your home. Set a regular calendar reminder to check if the included items have expired. Items to put in your first-aid kit include:

- Names and numbers of your regular vet clinic, emergency animal hospital, and poison control
- Leash
- Towel/blanket
- Bandage material (gauze squares, sterile nonstick pads, gauze wrap, vet wrap, bandage tape, tongue depressors, and bandage scissors)
- Corn syrup (for combating low blood sugar)
- 3% hydrogen peroxide
- Nail clippers and tweezers
- Penlight/flashlight
- Rectal thermometer and lubricant
- Gloves
- Muzzle
- Antibacterial soap
- Sterile rinse (saline)
- Rubbing alcohol
- Clean syringes

Licking Sores

Lick granulomas, or licking sores, are a form of self-injury caused by repeatedly licking the same area. It is important to determine the trigger of the licking—usually pain, itchiness from allergies, or psychological factors. Preventing further licking and subsequent trauma is critical to healing these injuries, so your dog may be required to wear a cone or sock to block access to the area. Your vet may also prescribe antibiotics if a secondary skin infection is present. If the licking is caused by a psychological factor, such as anxiety or stress, the only way to manage this issue is to identify and remove the triggers or work toward modifying the behavior. Behavioral medications can help reduce severe anxiety while you come up with a behavior modification plan.

Coneheads

If your puppy has a surgical procedure or injury, they may have to wear a special kind of collar to keep them from licking their wounds, which delays the healing process and can lead to infection. The most common one is a big plastic cone called an E-collar (short for "Elizabethan collar," because it's reminiscent of the large ruffled collars worn in Elizabethan England). However, if your puppy hates the "cone of shame," there are other less intrusive alternatives. These include inflatable collars (that resemble a neck pillow or "donut"), a soft collar (similar to a regular cone but made of softer fabric instead of hard plastic), or even a T-shirt or puppy onesie that covers the injury.

Any time you're testing out one of these methods, supervise your dog at first to make sure it actually prevents licking. You might be surprised how quickly your puppy finds a workaround! You may feel inclined to remove your dog's cone or chosen apparatus for bathroom breaks and eating, which is fine as long as you're actively supervising your puppy the entire time. Be sure to modify your puppy's environment or access if you need to leave them alone with their cone on—you don't want them to smash into things and damage your home or themselves.

Upset Tummy

An upset tummy can take the form of anything from gas to diarrhea to vomiting to refusal to eat. Upset tummies are common but can be caused by many different factors. Common culprits for indigestion include eating new or rich foods (often scraps of human food), swallowing foreign items, parasites, or bacterial infections. Determining what caused your puppy's upset tummy will help you prevent a relapse in the future. If it was caused by introducing a new diet, you'll need to make the transition more gradual, or perhaps the new food is not appropriate for your dog.

It's always best to contact your vet if your puppy is show-ing signs of an upset tummy, as they'll be able to advise you best on how to monitor and treat it. With vomiting, you may be advised not to let your puppy eat anything for 12 to 24 hours, but you must be careful in young or very small puppies, as their blood sugar can drop quickly without food. If diarrhea is the main symptom, it's often advisable to feed small, frequent portions of either a bland dog food or home-cooked rice and boiled chicken. A bland, easily digestible diet may be enough to give your puppy's tummy the break it needs to recover. Some episodes of indigestion may require medications, so again, it's best to contact your vet.

Scooting

A dog "scooting" their bum across the floor can be a sign of worms, but more often it indicates issues with the dog's anal glands. The anal glands are located inside the rectum and secrete a smelly, oily substance that is thought to be an identification or territorial marker. When your dog has a bowel movement, the pressure of the passing stool on the glands causes them to excrete this substance. This is usually enough to keep the glands flaccid, but some dogs have trouble emptying their glands. When the glands become full, impacted, or infected, your dog might rub their bum along the ground to try and alleviate the itching and irritation. Luckily, glands can be expressed easily by your veterinary staff or groomer. With some instruction, you can even learn how to empty them at home (if you have the stomach for it). Leaving a dog with full anal glands can cause infection or rupture, so if you notice your dog scooting, it's time for a visit to the vet.

Ear Infections

Though ear mites can be a culprit in puppies, the most common cause of canine ear infections is yeast. Naturally occurring yeast can overgrow in the ear canal, producing a thick, greasy, brown or gray discharge and an unpleasant odor. Your dog will scratch, rub, or shake its ears to try to alleviate the itch. This can result in inflamed ears, thickened tissue, secondary infection, and trauma to the earflap. Your vet can run tests and prescribe antimicrobials and anti-inflammatories if necessary. Often, you'll be instructed to clean your dog's ears regularly with

a prescription ear wash (see page 101), and if the ear infections are chronic and repetitive, you may want to discuss diet changes with your vet, as this can be a sign of food allergies.

Health by Breed

Certain dog breeds are more likely to have certain health problems. This is more common in purebred dogs but affects mixed breeds, as well. Be sure to research your dog's breed so that you're prepared for common health problems. Here is a (non-exhaustive) list of some of the most common problems experienced by a selection of more common breeds.

BREED	HEALTH ISSUE
Australian shepherd	Hearing loss or deafness, epilepsy, cataracts, moderate to severe allergies, hip dysplasia, cancer (lymphoma and hemangiosarcoma)
Beagle	Epilepsy, spine issues, eye issues, hip dysplasia, hypothyroidism
Bichon frise	Liver problems, bladder stones, allergies, gum disease, ear infections, cataracts, diabetes, wobbly kneecaps, Cushing's syndrome
Boston terrier	Cataracts, blindness, deafness, skin allergies, breathing issues
Boxer	Heart conditions, allergies, higher risk of cancer
Bulldog	Skin fold dermatitis, hip dysplasia, eye issues (including cherry eye), breathing issues

BREED	HEALTH ISSUE
Cavalier King Charles spaniel	Heart disease, spine problems, hip dysplasia, deafness, cherry eye
Chihuahua	Collapsing trachea (throat), dental disease, hypoglycemia, wobbly kneecaps
Cocker spaniel	Ear infections and disorders, eye issues
Corgi	Spinal cord disease, dental disease, spine problems
Dachshund	Spine and back problems, eye issues, skin problems, dental disease, Cushing's syndrome
Dalmatian	Deafness, epilepsy, copper storage disease
Doberman pinscher	Heart issues, bleeding disorder, hypothyroidism, bloat
French bulldog	Back/spine disorders, allergies
German shepherd	Hip dysplasia, bloat, growing pains, anal infections, spinal cord disease
German short-haired pointer	Heart disorders, epilepsy, hip dysplasia, eye conditions
Golden retriever	Cataracts, blindness, skin issues, hypothyroidism, bloat, cancer
Great Dane	Bloat, heart issues, eye conditions, growing pains, deafness, "wobbler syndrome"

BREED	HEALTH ISSUE
Labrador retriever	Obesity, joint disease, eye conditions, allergies, ear infections, heart disease, throat paralysis, cancer
Miniature schnauzer	Diabetes, pancreatitis, epilepsy, bladder stones
Pomeranian	Heart disease, collapsing trachea, cataracts, alopecia X ("black skin disease"), spine problems
Poodle	Bloat, Addison's disease, epilepsy, hypothyroidism, skin disease, eye conditions
Pug	Eye conditions (including eye prolapse), breathing issues, skin issues, brain disease
Rottweiler	Elbow/hip dysplasia, splenic tumors, heart issues, eyelid issues, bone cancer
Shih tzu	Wobbly kneecaps, eye issues, dental disease, breathing issues, heat intolerance, back and neck problems
Siberian husky	Autoimmune disorders, skin disease, eye problems, hip dysplasia
Yorkshire terrier	Liver shunt, hypoglycemia, eye issues, collapsing trachea, wobbly kneecaps, pancreatitis, dental disease, skin allergies, hip problems

When to Call the Vet

Sometimes your puppy's health problems will need to be handled by a professional, but it can be difficult to know what counts as an emergency. If you're ever in doubt, go ahead and call your vet or emergency vet clinic. They're trained to ask the questions necessary to assess the problem at hand. They won't think you're being silly or overreacting; they'll appreciate your proactive approach.

Some common veterinary emergencies are:

- ingesting something toxic
- swallowing foreign bodies
- dehydration
- collapse
- bloody vomit/diarrhea
- trauma (e.g., being hit by a car, injured in a dog fight, etc.)
- seizures
- pale, blue, or bright red gums (they should be a nice salmon-pink color)
- straining or inability to urinate
- vomiting and/or diarrhea that is frequent or lasts longer than 24 hours
- eye trauma/concerns (never wait to call about eyes, as potential consequences include blindness)

Some ailments that might be okay to leave until the following day are:

- ear infections
- acute/infrequent diarrhea
- itchy red skin
- scooting
- decreased appetite (acute)
- parasites
- mild, acute cough

Familiarize yourself with your puppy's normal resting heart rate, respiration rate, and temperature, which your veterinary team can guide you in assessing. This will help you share the right information with your vet over the phone during a potential emergency.

CHAPTER 7

Raising a Happy Puppy

You don't just want to raise a healthy puppy—you want to raise a happy, friendly, well-behaved puppy, too. A lot of these factors are greatly affected by how you handle your puppy in their early months. This chapter will cover how to raise a well-adjusted dog.

Socialization

Socializing your puppy is an important responsibility. It helps ensure that your dog becomes a good citizen, gets along well with humans and other animals, and handles unexpected situations with confidence. Socialization is often misunderstood and improperly executed—but this section is designed to set you and your puppy up for social success!

What Is Socialization?

Socializing is how an animal learns to interact with members of its own species, animals of other species, and novel stimuli and environments. It's not just about exposure in and of itself—your puppy needs to have *positive* experiences. Frightening experiences can result in fear that lasts throughout your dog's life, but using treats and praise helps your puppy create a positive association with novel stimuli, boosting their confidence and social skills. Practice patience with your puppy and allow them to approach and explore at their own pace. Learn to recognize body language that indicates fear or uncertainty so you can offer your puppy more support or an exit strategy. Socialization is not a passive process; you need to be actively involved, teaching your puppy that the world isn't a scary place.

Why Is Socialization Important?

Puppies who don't receive adequate and appropriate socialization when they're young tend to be fearful of unfamiliar people, animals, sounds, objects, and environments. This fear can lead to further issues, such as aggression. Biting is a normal response for a fearful dog, but if it gets really bad, it can lead to rehoming—or worse, you may be compelled to put your dog down. In fact, according to the American Veterinary Society of Animal Behavior (AVSAB), behavioral issues are not just "the number one cause of relinquishment to shelters" but also "the number one cause of death for dogs under three years of age." Socialization will help prevent your dog from experiencing such an intense level of fear that they feel the need to fight.

The good news is that there are a ton of different ways you can help avoid behavioral issues in your puppy and even modify existing problematic behaviors. On top of that, socialization will teach your dog to be polite and easy to get along with. Training your dog on manners and tricks can be done at any stage of life, but since socialization has a finite period for maximum efficacy, this should be a top priority from the get-go.

When and Where Does Socialization Happen?

From roughly 3 to 12 weeks of age (possibly extending to 14 or 16 weeks), your puppy is in what's called the "socialization period." During this time, a puppy's curiosity often outweighs their fear, making it the best time for them to adapt to other animals, new people, and unfamiliar environments. Puppies in their social period are also primed for bonding with other animals and people and for learning that objects, people, and environments are safe. They are also best able to learn others' body cues and signals, what they mean, and how to respond. Socialization is so important that AVSAB believes it should be standard for puppies to start even before they're fully vaccinated. While puppies' immune systems are not fully protected yet, a combination of antibodies from their mother, introductory vaccinations, and appropriate care will help protect them from disease.

Ideally, socialization begins with the breeder, while your puppy is still with their mom and littermates. Socialization

classes are also recommended for puppies as early as seven to eight weeks of age (so long as their first vaccination has been administered seven days prior to starting the class—be sure the instructor enforces a vaccine policy). These classes can offer a safe, controlled environment with a minimal risk of illness.

And, of course, socialization happens with you! Once your puppy is vaccinated, bring them out into the world with you and aim to expose them to all that they may encounter later in life. Let's take a closer look at how to do that.

Socialization Step by Step

Socializing your puppy can be a daunting task, especially since it's so crucial to raising a healthy dog. Here are seven steps you can take to set your puppy up for successful socialization.

1. **Prioritize potty breaks.** When taking your puppy to a new place, such as a friend's house, make sure to let them eliminate before bringing them inside and take a proactive approach to bathroom breaks once you're inside.

2. **Keep it positive.** Treats, praise, a favorite toy, playtime—these are great ways to get your puppy to associate good things with whatever you're introducing them to.

3. **Go slow.** Never rush or force your puppy to investigate something when they're unsure. If you do, your puppy might associate stress and fear with the stimulus, which can carry a lasting impression through to adulthood—the exact opposite of what you want! Be patient and let your puppy set the pace.

4. **Start small.** Introduce your puppy to one new person at a time rather than a large group. Remember that it may take a couple of repeat exposures before your puppy is happily interacting with something new, and that's okay!

Socialization Scavenger Hunt

The following are all things I recommend exposing your puppy to in a controlled and positive manner. (But remember, this list is not all-inclusive. There are no limits to socializing.)

- [ ] Handling (touching different body parts, gently restraining your puppy, putting on their collar, etc.)
- [ ] Unfamiliar people (people of all different ages, genders, and ethnicities, with different kinds of clothes or accessories such as hats, sunglasses, backpacks, and canes)
- [ ] Other dogs (dogs of different ages who play well)
- [ ] Other animals (cats, livestock, other pets, etc.)
- [ ] Unfamiliar surfaces (concrete, slippery floors, metal surfaces, stairs, grass, mud, ice, snow, etc.)
- [ ] Potentially scary sounds (babies and kids, alarms, doorbells, other dogs barking, traffic, vacuums, sirens, etc.)
- [ ] Potentially scary objects (pots and pans, brooms, balloons, umbrellas, etc.)
- [ ] Wheeled objects (skateboards, strollers, wheelchairs, bikes, motor vehicles, etc.)
- [ ] New environments, once fully vaccinated (residential neighborhoods, city streets, parking lots, new buildings, dog-friendly events and businesses, being home alone, etc.)

5. **Take control.** Set up situations you have control over. Always have an exit strategy in case things start to go badly.

6. **Stay calm.** If your puppy shows signs of fear or uncertainty, use gentle encouragement and support, coupled with treats, to help them through their nerves. If your puppy acts fearful, take a few steps back until you notice a shift in their body language—there's always next time to get closer! If you feel anxious or unsettled, your puppy can pick up on it and develop uncertainty about the situation.

7. **Hire a professional.** Puppy classes are a great opportunity for your puppy to meet new people and dogs and to practice play with a group. It's also a great place for you to ask questions and build your own confidence. (See page 165 for more information on puppy classes.)

Common Behavior Concerns

Just like humans, puppies can have emotional issues. This might happen because the puppy wasn't well socialized in their early days, because of certain traumatic events, or because they genetically inherited certain traits from their parents—or it might just be an individual quirk. These problems can be stressful for a pet owner, but this section will teach you how to address them. And if you're ever concerned or overwhelmed with your puppy's behavior, contact a professional for assistance.

Separation Anxiety

Separation anxiety occurs when your dog experiences stress or even a full-on panic attack when left alone. Symptoms include going to the bathroom in the house; destroying property, particularly exits to rooms or crates during attempts

Behavior Modification Methods

Desensitization is, as psychologist and dog trainer Zazie Todd puts it, a "very gradual exposure to the scary thing, starting at a very low level and building up very slowly." For example, if your dog is worried about being left alone, place them in their confinement area, walk to a different room for one second, then return. Next time, do five seconds, then ten seconds, and so on, gradually increasing the length of time you're away. The key to successful desensitization is keeping your puppy happy and comfortable during the process. If they show signs of fear, you could actually be *sensitizing* your dog and making the problem worse.

Classical conditioning is the process of pairing a neutral stimulus with a potent reinforcement for the animal (like treats). The goal of this technique is to teach your dog to associate the stimulus with positive emotions.

Counterconditioning is the same process as classical conditioning, but for a negative stimulus rather than a neutral one. Counterconditioning is often employed in conjunction with desensitization to overcome fear in dogs.

A replacement behavior is a desirable behavior you teach a dog to do in place of an undesired one. For example, if you don't want your puppy to bark when the doorbell rings, you can teach them to grab a plush toy instead.

to escape; self-harm, usually as a result of this destruction; excessive vocalization, such as whimpering, barking, or howling; and refusal to eat when alone. You might also notice that your dog shows signs of anxiety when you're getting ready to leave the house, such as following you around, panting, pacing, and vocalizing. Over time, your puppy can start to learn your routine, and something as simple as brushing your teeth might trigger them to stick to you like Velcro or exhibit other signs of stress. Your puppy may become hyper-vigilant, constantly searching for signs that you might be leaving them, resulting in a vicious cycle of stress and worry. The American Veterinary Medical Association estimates that 20 percent of all dogs suffer from some degree of separation anxiety.

Separation anxiety will not resolve itself. If you suspect your puppy is dealing with any degree of separation anxiety, try giving them a treat or stuffed Kong when you place them in their confinement area or crate before you go. Be sure to

downplay your departures and arrivals, avoiding prolonged goodbyes and overly excited greetings. If the problem doesn't resolve or is severe to begin with, consult with a certified positive-reinforcement dog trainer as well as your veterinarian. Gradually desensitizing your puppy to departures will help teach your dog to be confident and comfortable when left alone. It's not uncommon for dogs experiencing separation anxiety to require antianxiety medications in conjunction with training, but medication alone will not solve the problem.

Shyness and Fearfulness

A fearful or shy puppy might act timid, skittish, or worried around anything novel, displaying a tucked tail, hunched posture, or flattened ears, or hiding or fleeing from the stimulus. They may be easily startled, and they can often take longer to become comfortable with novel stimuli or recover from a fright. Fear can be classified as normal or abnormal, depending on the context. For example, if another dog attacked your

Bait and Switch

If your puppy manages to get an item that is not puppy-safe (e.g., garbage, your shoe, or something toxic), you may need to employ the "bait and switch" technique. This is not quite the same as counterconditioning; it's more of an emergency measure to quickly and safely get something away from your puppy. Here's how bait and switch works.

- Offer your puppy a treat they value more than the item they currently have. For example, if the puppy is chewing on a sock, you might offer them a small piece of chicken.
- When the puppy opens their mouth to accept the treat, calmly remove the forbidden object from their possession. (The object will often drop as the puppy opens their mouth to take the treat.)
- Feed your puppy the high-value treat. Dispose of the item or put it away where the puppy can't get it.

Try rehearsing the technique when your puppy is chewing on a lower-value toy, just so you can get comfortable with the mechanics and your puppy can get used to happily giving you items from their mouth.

puppy, it would be normal for them to be scared. But if a person came into sight 50 feet away and your puppy reacted by screaming and scrambling away, that would be an abnormal fear response.

If your puppy is displaying fear, it's important to address it appropriately. If you don't recognize and respect a dog's fear, it can escalate to aggression. The best way to respond is with counterconditioning. For example, every time your puppy perceives a vacuum, you start babbling in an upbeat voice and feeding them a continuous stream of chicken. As your puppy develops happy emotions about the vacuum, you can start to move the vacuum closer to them, turn it on, and so forth. By doing this gradually, at an intensity your puppy is comfortable with, you can effectively teach your puppy that a once-scary item is safe. Let your puppy dictate their own progress and never rush them or force them to interact with something they're unsure about. Should your puppy display any signs of fear or uncertainty, stop what you're doing and decrease the intensity.

If your puppy is displaying generalized fear at a young age, or even after repeated positive exposures, it's best to consult with a professional dog trainer so they can help pinpoint your puppy's triggers, build a gradual desensitization plan, and provide support and feedback during the training process.

Resource Guarding

Resource guarding is when a puppy tries to prevent anyone from taking away items it finds valuable, such as food, bones, treats, toys, stolen items, or even people. They may do this by growling, freezing, giving a hard stare, gulping or inhaling their food, snarling, lunging, or biting. Overall, it's a normal behavior that dogs have retained from their wolf ancestors—who needed it to survive—but it's one we humans don't like to see.

Commonly, we feel like we should try to "dominate" or withhold resources from a dog who does this, but these solutions can make the problem worse. A better method is to change how the puppy views your approach to them and their stuff. Instead of viewing you as a threat to their possessions, use counterconditioning to show your puppy that your approach is a good thing.

Let's say your puppy resource-guards their food bowl. Start with an empty food bowl. Approach and add a handful of kibble. Repeat this process over the course of a few days until they're comfortable with it. Then start waiting until the puppy is eating and has a few pieces of kibble left, approach, and add another handful of kibble. Repeat this process until the puppy is comfortable with it (which might take days). Next, when your puppy is eating their regular meal, approach and add a higher-value reward, such as chicken or hot dog. Once your puppy is comfortable with that, try approaching during mealtime, touching the bowl, and adding the high-value reward. Eventually, your puppy will learn that it's a good thing for you to be near them when they're eating.

You can also help prevent resource guarding before it starts by reducing conflict around resources. Feed your puppy in a quiet area away from kids and other pets to reduce potential stress during mealtimes. Give your puppy bones or other chews in these quiet areas or in their crate. If necessary, consult with a certified positive-reinforcement trainer to help you rehabilitate resource guarding appropriately and safely.

Aggression

Aggression is a label that can loosely be applied to almost anything, from growling and snarling to snapping and biting. Identifying true aggression can be tricky, as these can also be signs of fear or just normal, healthy puppy play. Even biting humans is not always aggression; it could be normal play with a lack of appropriate bite inhibition. For this reason, it's extremely important to evaluate the context of any aggressive behavior as well as the puppy's body language. Overall tension (e.g., stiff body, legs, tail, head, etc.) usually indicates aggression rather than fear or playfulness.

Aggressive behaviors become a concern if they're abnormally intense, frequent, or long-lasting. If a 12-week-old puppy responded to a vet examining their mouth by growling and snapping repeatedly, for example, that would be considered an abnormal reaction. The more your puppy practices these behaviors, the more challenging it becomes to modify them, so try to identify what's triggering the behavior and prevent your puppy from being exposed to it. For example, if your puppy growls at you when you pick them up to move them while they're sleeping, stop doing that! Instead, try leading them gently with a leash or luring them with treats to teach them to move from one spot to another. Otherwise, they'll just keep rehearsing the aggressive behavior, and it will get more and more entrenched.

If you're worried about aggressive behavior or are witnessing behavior like this regularly from a young puppy, speak with a professional dog trainer as soon as possible! What might be easy to manage when they're small quickly becomes a safety concern as they grow.

Jumping Up

Our dogs jump up on us to gain access and attention. Often, when people are approached by a young puppy who jumps, they respond with petting and attention. This reaction reinforces the puppy's choice and will result in them jumping up again in the future—after all, it worked well for them in the past! To prevent your puppy from jumping on visitors, you'll need to remove any reinforcement for the behavior. This means coaching anyone greeting your puppy not to pay any attention unless the puppy has all four feet on the ground.

Alternatively, you can pretrain your dog to "Sit" and cue this behavior whenever you encounter someone new. The puppy's sit can be rewarded by attention from the stranger, which is what the dog wanted in the first place. This is called a "replacement behavior" (see page 124), and you can use it to replace any undesirable behavior.

If your puppy has a habit of jumping on you when you let them out of their crate or return home at the end of the day, try to ignore them until their feet are firmly placed on the ground. If your puppy is persistent and jumps up on you repeatedly even when being ignored, remove the puppy's access to you. When the puppy jumps up, promptly tell it "Too bad" and leave the room. If you're coming in the front door, turn around and exit the house, closing the door behind you. If you're already inside the house, you can step into another room, such as the bathroom, and close the door. By removing yourself from the situation, you're also removing the puppy's opportunity for attention. Be consistent and implement these "time-outs" every time your puppy jumps.

Chewing

Chewing is a completely normal and healthy puppy behavior, so it's important to provide your puppy with plenty of approved chewing outlets and opportunities rather than trying to smother their desire to chew. Chew treats (page 50), chew toys (page 56), and interactive feeding (page 61) are great ways to accomplish this.

The best way to prevent inappropriate chewing is to actively supervise your puppy while they're loose in the house. If you can't, place the puppy in their crate or other confined area with a chew toy to prevent them from making a mistake and chewing something they're not supposed to. When you leave your puppy alone for the day, some degree of confinement will likely be necessary to prevent destruction. Proactively help your dog make successful choices by managing the environment and supervising your puppy when you're home.

Excessive Barking

Barking is a form of communication and can occur for a multitude of reasons. Knowing the motivation behind the behavior is important in determining how to address it. Here are a few different types of barking your puppy may exhibit.

Demand barking. Your puppy might bark at you if they want something, such as attention or playtime. If you respond by, say, throwing a ball, you've just accidentally taught your puppy that barking for attention works. When your puppy demand-barks, it's best to ignore them until they're quiet, then reward the silence with play or another interaction. You've now reinforced the behavior you want. Alternatively, you can ask your dog for a different, more appropriate behavior in place of barking, such as sitting, when it wants attention from you.

Barking when alone. This can be one of many signs that your dog has separation anxiety. If your puppy is truly panicking (not just having a temper tantrum), you should address this issue promptly and carefully (see page 123).

Barking out of boredom. Bored puppies often entertain themselves in ways we don't enjoy, such as barking at birds in the yard. If your puppy is doing this, you'll need to alleviate their boredom. Find ways to stimulate your dog mentally and physically—and to tire them out (see chapter 4 for ideas).

Fear barking. A puppy who is startled or afraid might bark as a way to say, "Give me space!" Barking out of fear is good communication and should be respected. It's important to identify what's causing the fearful response and to address it using the techniques on page 124.

Alert barking. Puppies who are doing their due diligence as guard dogs will bark to alert you to the presence of someone or something, often at the front door or in the yard. If your dog is a window watcher, blocking the visual stimulation with curtains can solve the problem immediately. If your puppy is alert-barking, ask yourself, "What would I like my puppy to do instead?" Then teach your puppy to do that. You might teach your puppy to recall to you instead of barking at squirrels or sit quietly at the top of the stairs when people come to the front door. Reward the behavior you like with treats and praise!

A Day in the Dog Park

Once your puppy is fully vaccinated, the dog park is a great place for them to socialize, exercise, and have fun. This section will discuss what to look for in a dog park and how to make the most of your experience there.

What to Look for in a Dog Park

A fenced park is ideal for keeping your puppy from running away while they're playing off-leash, especially if they don't yet have a reliable recall! Fences can also keep your dog safe from nearby traffic. Double-gated entry and exit points are great at preventing accidental escapes as well as issues with crowding at gates. A dog park should be large—at least one acre for large breeds—to provide ample space for the dogs to run around (and avoid dogs they don't want to be around). An oddly shaped piece of land makes for more environmental stimulation, as do trees and other foliage. Hills are great because they can encourage dogs to slow down while they're running and chasing each other, whereas flat ground more easily permits flat-out sprinting and body checking that can quickly escalate into higher-intensity play. Hiding places and barriers (natural or artificial) are good to break up play and slow dogs down. For small dogs, try to choose a park with a designated small-dog area. This keeps your puppy safe from being unintentionally rolled, frightened, or injured by larger playmates.

Dog Park Etiquette

Dogs should be off-leash in a dog park. A leash can not only be a frustrating barrier for dogs trying to interact with each other, it can also prevent them from avoiding dogs they don't get along with and negatively impact communication between them. If your dog is not good off-leash around other dogs, then dog parks are not the right choice for you.

You should have an idea of basic dog body language before visiting the dog park so you can recognize signs of stress, fear, and aggression, but most dogs can sort out minor conflicts on their own. For example, "snarking" (giving a warning growl to other dogs) is simply a form of communication; it's how dogs say, "No thank you," or "Don't do that," and they should be permitted to voice their boundaries so long as these conversations don't result in any injuries.

If you're worried that your dog is playing too roughly or is the victim of rough play, perform a consent test (see page 64). If your puppy is persistently harassing or bullying another dog in the park, leash your puppy and remove them from the off-leash area for a 15-minute "time-out." If the inappropriate behavior recurs following this time-out, remove your puppy from the park. These negative consequences will hopefully prompt them to be more respectful at their next visit.

Dog Park Precautions

Dog parks are a great source of exercise, socialization, and fun, but between communal drinking bowls, shared toys, and the presence of poop from a bunch of different dogs, they can also be a breeding ground for parasites and diseases. If you plan on frequenting dog parks, make sure your puppy is up to date on vaccines (including Bordetella), preventive medications, their deworming schedule, and so on. Additionally, dogs that haven't been spayed or neutered shouldn't go to dog parks. An intact dog can cause intense interest and fighting behaviors, not to mention accidental pregnancies.

When You're Not Home

Being home with your puppy 24/7 isn't realistic—who doesn't go to work, school, or social events sometimes? This section is about what to do with your puppy when life's obligations take you away from home.

Home Alone

All puppies will need to learn that being alone sometimes is a normal part of life. Most puppies need to be confined when they're alone—in a crate, exercise pen, or puppy-proofed bathroom or laundry room—both to keep them safe and to prevent mischief. It's important to teach your puppy to be comfortable in their confinement area for as long as you'll be away *before* you start leaving them alone for the day (see page 149 for information on crate training, and then adjust for the confinement area of your choice if necessary).

Take your puppy for a potty break directly before you confine them. Puppies can generally hold their bladder the same number of hours as their age in months, so a three-month-old puppy can only go three hours before needing a potty break. Even when your puppy is older and fully potty-trained, I would recommend a maximum of four hours in the crate (aside from sleeping through the night). While your puppy may technically be able to hold their bladder longer than that, they still need a chance to stretch their legs and burn off some energy. If your workday doesn't allow you to come home midday to let your puppy out, employ the help of a friend, neighbor, or dog walker.

Doggy Daycare

Doggy daycare is just what it sounds like: a place where people can drop off their dogs during the day. This is an excellent option if you, say, can't get home from work during a midday break or can't sufficiently exercise your puppy before or after work. Depending on your dog's feeding needs, you may or may not need to send their "lunch" with them. Daycare fees can range from around $25 to $50 a day, with most centers offering monthly rates. When searching for the perfect daycare, remember: You get what you pay for. While a cheaper daycare may be kinder on the pocketbook, ask yourself how they afford it. Do they have a smaller staff? Have they cut costs on cleaning and maintenance?

   Here are some things to keep in mind when choosing a doggy daycare.

▶ **What are the vaccination requirements?** Daycare is only an appropriate option for fully vaccinated puppies. They should only allow dogs that have all their vaccinations, including kennel cough (Bordetella).

▶ **How transparent are they?** They should allow you to tour the facility, view the dogs during working hours, and watch how the employees interact with the dogs and how they allow the dogs to interact with one another.

Calming Aids

Anxiety is a normal emotional response, and at low levels, it helps keep your puppy safe. But in extra stressful situations, such as travel, boarding, vet visits, thunderstorms, or holidays with fireworks, you may want to find some calming aids to help comfort your puppy. One option is calming treats, which contain naturally relaxing ingredients such as melatonin, L-theanine, tryptophan, and derivatives of proteins found in mother's milk. Another option is the ThunderShirt, a popular piece of clothing that soothes a dog by applying constant gentle pressure, kind of like swaddling a baby. You can also try simple background noise or music. One study found that some dogs prefer soft rock and reggae music, but music in general can keep a dog's mind occupied on something other than the stressor. If your dog has moderate or severe anxiety, speak with your vet about working with a certified trainer or even potentially using antianxiety medication.

▶ **What is their policy on quiet time for dogs?** Do they implement breaks for the dogs, and if so, do they provide these at certain times of the day or when they feel the dogs need one? How do they determine when a dog needs a break? It's preferable if your daycare has two separate areas: one for quieter, older, smaller, or more timid dogs, and one for the younger, busier, larger, or more rambunctious dogs.

▶ **What are their handling and training methods?** Do they use aversives, such as spray bottles or noise cans, for barking dogs, or are they committed to positive-reinforcement techniques? What sort of training do their employees have regarding dog body language and play? How do they break up a fight, and how do they handle the offending dogs moving forward? Do they have an injury protocol if a dog gets hurt?

▶ **What is their employee-to-dog ratio?** An ideal ratio is 8 dogs per 1 human, and certainly no more than 15 dogs per 1 human.

Hire a Dog Walker

Dog walkers come to your home and walk your dog when you can't. Like doggy daycare, they're a great option for people who can't provide that afternoon potty break because of work or can't meet their puppy's exercise needs on their own. Dog walkers might walk your pet around your neighborhood or transport them to another location to walk them. Walks can be done individually or in groups, depending on the services your walker offers and what you'd prefer. They might be self-employed, or they might work for a company.

When looking for a dog walker, choose one who is licensed and insured. While walking a dog may seem like a simple task,

a lot can happen, so be sure to ask about the walker's experience level during the interview process. Hiring someone who is trained in pet first aid can provide additional peace of mind. A dog walker can cost anywhere from $30 to $40 per hour, but that can vary greatly. It may be cheaper to have your dog walked in an off-leash group setting versus a private leash walk, so be sure to ask about the cost of various services.

Travel Plans

When adding a puppy to your family, it's best not to bring them home right before a trip, as this can interfere with those early days of bonding, socializing, and training. Once your dog becomes integrated into your family, however, you may want or need to travel. Here are a few options to consider when that happens.

Hire a Dog Sitter

A dog sitter, much like a house sitter, takes care of your puppy at your home while you're out of town. It's best to hire someone who will actually stay at your house (including overnight) for the duration of your trip rather than just stop by to feed and walk the dog. One of the bonuses of a dog sitter is that your puppy gets to remain in a familiar space and maintain a close-to-normal routine.

Finding potential friends or family members who may be interested in the position is a great place to start, but there are businesses that offer this service as well. Interview a new dog sitter the same way you would interview a new dog walker. Check on their experience, training (particularly in pet first aid), and licensing, if applicable.

Before leaving your puppy with a dog sitter, arrange for them to meet your puppy. This is also a great time to show the sitter your home and where to find all the necessary supplies. Make sure you have an ample supply of dog food, treats, and any medications your dog might be taking; running out of ear drops can be a big hassle when you're not home!

Leave a detailed list of instructions for the sitter, including the following:

▶ **Phone numbers,** including your cell phone, regular vet clinic, emergency vet clinic, and an emergency contact if the sitter can't reach you.

▶ **Feeding instructions** such as when and how much to feed, plus any special instructions. (Do you feed using interactive toys or puzzles? Does the puppy get fed in their crate or in a specific room?)

▶ **Any learned cues** that your puppy knows for eliminating, etc.

▶ **The names of any medications**, when and how much to give, how you administer them, etc.

▶ **Legal toys** your puppy is allowed to play with. Be sure to mention if certain toys require supervision.

▶ **Treats or chews** your puppy can have, how often to give them, and whether they require supervision (e.g., for chews and other long-lasting treats).

▶ **Your puppy's exercise routine,** including when, where, and how long to walk them; what equipment to use; and any other information (e.g., is the puppy allowed to greet people and/or dogs they encounter on walks?).

▶ **What to do when leaving the puppy alone for the day.** This might include a crate cue, how long the puppy can be left alone, your pre-departure routine (if any), etc.

Boarding at a Kennel

While you're traveling, your dog can also stay at a boarding facility, kennel, or "doggy hotel." Unfortunately, facilities are commonly full of barking dogs and quite noisy, which can cause overexcitement or stress. Your puppy likely won't receive the amount of human contact and individual attention they're used to. If you're considering boarding your puppy, schedule a single overnight stay to see how they do before making your final decision.

Before booking your puppy's stay, tour the facility, including all indoor and outdoor areas. The facility should be comfortable and have appropriate temperature control, ventilation, and lighting. Make sure the facility is clean and safe and has appropriate fencing and secure kennels. (If you're unsure, ask about their cleaning policies.) Ask how often a human is present at the facility in a 24-hour period, as well as all the same questions you'd ask a doggy daycare (see page 138).

Note that a boarding facility is not an option unless your puppy is fully vaccinated. Any facility that doesn't require full vaccinations (including kennel cough) is putting your puppy at high risk of contracting an illness and is best avoided.

Puppy on the Go

Perhaps your travel arrangements make it possible to bring your puppy along. While this reduces the hassle of making alternative arrangements for them, you'll have to do some planning to ensure a successful trip. First, consider your puppy's personality. Are they confident and curious or timid and shy? Will your puppy be able to adapt to and enjoy the trip, or will it cause a lot of additional stress and anxiety for both of you? Second, make sure your puppy is fully vaccinated, as you may be unable to control environmental exposure while out and about. Additionally, not all hotels or campgrounds are pet friendly, so research where you're staying beforehand to avoid any surprises.

If you do decide to bring your puppy with you on a trip, make sure they have a microchip or other form of permanent ID as well as a legible tag on their collar or harness with your contact information. Pack enough food to last the whole trip, plus extra in case you run into unplanned delays. It's not advisable to feed your puppy different food while on the road, as this sudden change can cause a tummy upset. You'll also need to bring food and water dishes; your puppy's bed and crate; and any medications, toys, and treats—so make sure you have room! If you're crossing any borders, check what paperwork is required for pets; you'll often be required to show proof of vaccination, including rabies. Last but not least, look up emergency veterinary clinics close to your destination before you depart so you're prepared for any unexpected injuries or illnesses.

CHAPTER 8

Basic Training

Though this is not a training book, this chapter will cover some of the basics you'll need to know in order to give your puppy the best possible care. Training your puppy will strengthen your bond by establishing clear communication, setting expectations, and developing manners to help your dog successfully navigate the world. You can apply similar techniques to commands not covered in this chapter, like "Sit," "Stay," "Lie down," and so on.

Positive Training

"Positive training," or "positive-reinforcement training," uses rewards and consequences to train a dog—*not* punishment. In this context, a consequence might be preventing your puppy's access to a person or reward (such as treats), but it is never painful, frightening, or intimidating. Positive training doesn't use "aversive techniques," such as physical reprimands or yelling, focusing instead on the animal's well-being.

In contrast, "aversive," or "traditional," training takes a "do it or else" approach. When the dog makes a mistake, this type of training uses corrections like yelling, leash "pops" or jerks, smacking the dog on the nose or rump, and pinching the dog's ear until it complies. Originally developed for military dogs, this technique can be very harsh and can quickly damage the bond and trust between you and your puppy. Science has shown that punishment slows down the learning process, as the learner can easily become withdrawn and hesitant for fear of getting something wrong. A dog who's afraid to get punished for doing the wrong thing is also afraid to try out the right thing.

Positive training is the preferred choice; it is respectful for both you and your puppy and focuses on relationship building through communication, clear criteria, rewards, and consequences. The puppy is free to learn through mistakes, as they don't have to fear punishment for guessing wrong. This results in a dog who is more engaged in their training and openly offers behaviors to you, which you can then reward if you approve or ignore if you don't!

Training Tips

Here are a few things to keep in mind as you use the positive training techniques in this chapter.

▶ By the time you take your puppy home at eight weeks old, they're fully capable of learning all the skills in this chapter. You can start teaching any of them as soon as you want. The most important ones to prioritize are crate training and potty training (which go hand in hand), as well as socialization (see page 118).

▶ A puppy who has just finished a meal will not work nearly as hard for treats as a puppy who is hungrily anticipating dinner. Training with your dog when they're hungry—and thus more motivated—can yield better results. Save your puppy's regular meal for after a training session, or, if your puppy loves their kibble, have them work for their meals during training sessions.

▶ Use high-value treats reserved specifically for training sessions. For maximum convenience, store them in a treat pouch that fastens around your waist and has a wide opening you can easily fit your hand into.

Crate Training

Crate training holds value for all puppies, even if you don't plan to crate them regularly. With positive training, you can teach your dog to enjoy the crate as a safe and secure place to rest in or move to when they're feeling overwhelmed. In addition, the crate is an extremely valuable tool to prevent destruction in the house and aid in potty training.

When to Start

You should start crate training with your puppy as soon as you bring them home—but you'll want to introduce the crate slowly. Rushing your puppy and asking them to be in their crate for too long, too soon, can make them hate the crate and set back your training. Remember that your puppy can only hold their bladder for one hour per month of age, limiting the length of time you can leave them in the crate.

What You'll Need

There are many styles and types of crates on the market, and each has its pros and cons.

Wire crate. This is usually my crate of choice. It's structured, but the puppy can see out of it, so it feels more open. These crates often come with a divider, which allows you to adjust the size of the crate based on the puppy's size as they grow. They also fold down flat for easier storage.

Plastic/hard-sided crate. These crates are also well structured, which makes escaping them more difficult. Their doors and "windows" have wire grating over them, so your puppy can still see out, but the space may seem a bit darker and smaller from the inside. They don't come with dividers, but you can use a box to adjust the size as needed. These crates can be taken apart into two pieces but won't store flat.

Soft/collapsible crate. These crates are great for traveling, as they can fold down flat and store easily. I wouldn't use a soft crate for training, though, because a determined puppy could escape very quickly. The doors usually close with a zipper, and if your puppy hasn't yet learned to comfortably wait, they may try to push through the entrance before you can zip it open or closed.

When determining the appropriate size for your puppy's crate, make sure there's enough room for them to stand up, turn around, and lie down comfortably. Any more space than that and you risk your puppy viewing the crate as having two separate halves: one to sleep in, and one to potty in. You can choose a crate size that fits your puppy as it currently stands, but don't forget that they're going to grow! To avoid upgrading your puppy's crate every month, choose one that's likely to fit your puppy when they're full-grown, then use a crate divider to adjust the size.

A comfortable mat or blanket to line the crate is nice, but don't leave your puppy alone with it if they have a habit of chewing fabrics, as this could result in them ingesting the materials. Durable chew toys like Kongs will keep your puppy occupied while you're increasing the duration of time they can successfully spend in the crate during crate training.

What to Do

You'll first want your puppy to be comfortable entering the crate. Throughout the day, place treats in the back of the crate for them to discover. They'll start to check out the crate for food more frequently, leading to a positive association. You can also feed your puppy meals, special treats, or chews in the crate.

With any training, keep your sessions short and sweet. Five- to fifteen-minute sessions work for most dogs, but watch for signs that your puppy is getting tired or overwhelmed, such as acting distracted, sniffing, walking away, or "quitting" on you. Crate training can be accomplished over just a few days if you train consistently several times a day and your puppy has no previous negative association with their crate. If you see potential signs of stress—whining, barking, panting, drooling, pawing, or chewing at the bars—stop what you're doing and go back to a step your puppy is comfortable with. They may just need to repeat an easier step a few more times before you increase your expectations.

Once your puppy is comfortable entering the crate, you'll want to teach them a cue that tells them when to go inside their crate. Choose a cue (e.g., "Kennel"), say it out loud, and immediately toss a treat into the crate. Praise your puppy for entering the crate to retrieve their treat. Repeat this exercise until your dog is quickly moving into the crate after you give your cue and toss the treat.

Next, give your cue ("Kennel") and hold on to the treat to see if your puppy will move into the crate on their own. When they do, praise them and feed them several treats in a row inside the crate. Repeat this step until your puppy is eagerly entering the crate following your verbal cue.

Now that your puppy is happily entering their crate when you give your cue, you'll want to teach them to stay in the crate for increasing periods of time. Start small: Cue your puppy into the crate and close the crate door for one second. Feed your puppy a treat through the side or top of the crate before opening the door and allowing them to exit. It's important to repeat this step several times to ensure that your puppy is happy and confident before asking for more from them. Gradually increase the length of time the crate door is shut: two seconds, three seconds, five seconds, and so on, making sure your dog is happy at each step of the process.

The next step is to start training for longer durations. You can do this by cueing your puppy into their crate and giving them a special chew toy or stuffed Kong to work on. Sit close by your puppy's crate while reading a book or watching TV and drop a tasty treat into the crate every two to three seconds. Continue for 10 minutes, then release your puppy from the crate.

As your puppy demonstrates success, begin to remove yourself from the picture. Once you've settled your puppy in the crate, get up and walk around the house. You can return every few seconds to drop a treat into the crate before leaving again. As you increase the length of time you leave your puppy in the crate (half an hour, one hour, two hours), you can space out your treat delivery until you're only dropping a treat in the crate every 5 to 10 minutes.

You are now ready to try some real departures! Once your puppy is settled in their crate, leave your house for 30 minutes. It can be helpful to set up a recording device to ensure that your puppy tolerates this without any stress before increasing your absence to an hour, two hours, and so on.

Potty Training

Potty training is the process of teaching your puppy where—and where *not*—to eliminate. When it comes to potty training, I'm a firm believer in setting your puppy up for success. Instead of waiting for them to make a mistake, prevent accidents from occurring in the first place and reward your puppy for eliminating in the appropriate area(s).

Generally, you'll want your puppy to eliminate outside of the house, though some owners may opt to train their dog to use absorbent pee pads (e.g., if they live in a top-floor condo and it's inconvenient to go outside frequently). If your end goal is to have a puppy who eliminates strictly outdoors, I would not recommend pee pads, as it just adds an additional step to your house-training process.

When to Start

Potty training should begin on day one! But remember: Your puppy has limited bladder control at first. A general rule is that a puppy can hold their bladder for one hour per month of age, which means a two-month-old puppy can hold their bladder for a *maximum* of two hours. Make sure you're not asking your puppy to go longer than physically possible between bathroom breaks, as that will only set your puppy up for failure and give you a mess to clean. As your puppy grows, they'll be able to hold their bladder for longer stretches.

What You'll Need

Before starting potty training, make sure you have all your supplies ready to go.

- ☐ **A designated potty spot.** Where in the yard will you take your puppy to eliminate? Everyone in the household should be clear about where this spot is so you can maintain consistency.

- ☐ **A leash and collar.** You'll use these when you take your puppy outside for bathroom breaks.

- ☐ **Treats.** These are rewards for successful elimination in the potty spot. Leave a container of treats next to your puppy's leash so you don't forget them on your outings.

- ☐ **Poop bags.** Bring these with you on walks so that you can clean up after your puppy. Tying a bag to your leash handle will ensure you're never caught without one!

- ☐ **An enzymatic cleaner.** This is a must-have for cleaning up any messes. Enzymatic cleaners break down pet odors so there is no residual smell that may attract your dog back to that spot in the future.

- ☐ **A confinement area.** A crate, small room, or exercise pen that your puppy is already familiar with will work. This area will be used to help "stretch" your puppy between bathroom breaks and teach them to hold their bladder longer.

What to Do

When you first start potty training, you'll need to provide your puppy with potty breaks frequently—every 30 to 90 minutes on average, depending on your puppy's age (remember: one hour for every month of age). Signs that your puppy may need to eliminate include circling, sniffing, whining, and suddenly stopping whatever they're doing.

When your puppy is transitioning from one activity to the next, be sure to provide a potty break in between. When your puppy wakes up from a nap, take them outside to eliminate. After they finish breakfast? Potty break. After a vigorous session of tug-of-war? You got it: potty break.

Take your puppy outside on a leash to their designated potty spot. Once there, stand quietly in one spot and allow your puppy to sniff around for five minutes. Should your puppy eliminate, make sure you shower them with treats and praise! After they've eliminated, let them off-leash to roam the yard (if it's safe) or proceed to take them on their walk.

If your puppy doesn't eliminate after five minutes in the potty spot, bring them back inside and place them in their confinement area for 30 minutes. The crate helps prevent the puppy from making a mistake and eliminating in the house; your puppy will be more reluctant to soil their bedding than to let loose while, say, playing in the kitchen. When 30 minutes are up, take them back outside to try again. Repeat this cycle until the puppy is successful at voiding outside.

When your puppy has eliminated, you can consider them "empty" and let them have some free time in the house. Free time still requires you to actively supervise your puppy, which means you need to be in the same room watching them. You may find this easier if you restrict how much of the house your puppy can access. Close the doors to rooms that are off-limits and use baby gates to prevent your puppy from wandering out of sight. Allow your puppy 30 minutes of free time before placing them in their crate or confinement area for another 15 to 30 minutes. Then head back outside and repeat the cycle all over again.

If your puppy has an accident in the house, don't panic or punish them. Just clean it up well using your enzymatic cleaner. If accidents are occurring regularly, try giving your puppy potty breaks more frequently and improving your "eyes-on" supervision so that you can quickly notice signs that your puppy needs to pee. When you tighten up your management of the puppy, you should notice a dramatic decrease in the number of accidents. Remember to be proactive, not reactive, and set your dog up to be successful!

Your puppy should more or less get the hang of things over the course of a few days, but I don't consider a puppy fully potty-trained until they go three weeks without an accident.

Recall Training

Teaching your dog to come when called is a very important behavior for safety reasons, and your puppy needs to be able to do it reliably before you attempt any off-leash walking, especially in unfenced areas or near roads. This can be an extremely difficult behavior for puppies to perform, as they're usually much more interested in sniffing, exploring, or playing than returning to their owners. But through recall training, you'll make coming when called very valuable for your puppy every time they do it.

When to Start

You can start recall training as soon as you bring your puppy home. Make sure to reserve ample time to teach this behavior before attempting any off-leash adventures. As you continue training your dog to come when called, you can practice training with varying distances and levels of environmental distraction. If you're consistent and train regularly, you can teach a reliable recall within a couple of weeks.

What You'll Need

To successfully train your dog to come when called, you'll need a few supplies.

- ☐ **A contained area or "long line" leash.** Start in an environment free of excessive distractions, like in your house or backyard. If you don't have access to a contained area, use a 20- to 30-foot "long line" leash, which gives your puppy some sense of freedom while still maintaining control and safety before their recall is reliable.

- ☐ **High-value treats.** As recall can be one of the most "expensive" behaviors for our dogs to perform (i.e., it's hard for them to give up doing something they like to come when they're called), I recommend reserving a special type of treat solely to reward this behavior. For example, if your puppy goes bananas for cheddar cheese, save your cheese cubes for recall training, and always ensure that you're well stocked before heading out into the yard or putting your dog on their long line in the forest.

- ☐ **A recall cue.** Decide what this will be before you start training. The most well-known cue for a recall is "Come," but if your puppy already has a history of ignoring this cue, I recommend changing to a new one.

What to Do

The first step to successful recall training is to teach your dog that coming to you when called pays off big-time. To start, when you're in the same room of the house as your puppy, give your recall cue (e.g., "Come") and follow it up with a lot of excitement and encouragement, prompting your puppy to come see what all the fuss is about. When your puppy reaches you, praise them lavishly and feed them several of their special high-value recall treats. Do this at random times throughout the day when your puppy is least expecting it.

If your puppy can readily run to you when you call them in the same room, try calling them from another room. Give your recall cue one time and follow it with excitement and prompting until your puppy finds you. Don't be stingy on the treats when they get to you.

Once your puppy successfully comes when called from various rooms in the house, try this process outside in a fenced backyard or in a quiet area on a long line. There are plenty of new distractions outside, so be prepared for your puppy to respond more slowly and need a lot more encouragement. Remember to pay handsomely when your puppy reaches you—this is hard work!

When your puppy can quickly and reliably recall to you in your yard, begin to branch out to newer, slightly more distracting environments to practice in. Add distractions into your training sessions gradually and only after your dog is successful in the current setting. The dog park shouldn't be the first place you attempt recalls outside of your yard, as it would be far too big a jump in difficulty. Remember, set your puppy up for success, and build on their triumphs.

Avoid repeating your recall cue multiple times. This is an excellent way to teach your puppy that the word "Come" means "Continue what you're currently doing." If your puppy doesn't respond to your cue, follow it up with encouragement and prompting such as clapping your hands, whistling, making kissy noises, or speaking in a high-pitched and enthusiastic voice.

Leash Training

Leash training is the process of teaching your puppy to walk politely on a leash without pulling. A leash is an important tool that allows your puppy to safely explore the world. When teaching leash training, I require a dog to maintain slack in the leash so that they're not actively pulling, but I don't worry so much about whether they're slightly ahead of or behind my leg. If the leash has slack and my dog is on the chosen side of my body, I'm happy.

I encourage owners to allow their dogs ample opportunity to sniff and explore during walks. After all, a walk is supposed to be for the dog, and sniffing and exploring are extremely valuable and enriching activities for them! This can be accomplished by using a cue like "Go sniff" that tells your puppy when they're allowed to sniff around, and a cue like "Let's go" that tells them when they need to walk politely with a loose leash.

When to Start

You can start leash training as early as you want. A leash will be employed during potty training, so ensuring that your puppy is comfortable on one will make potty breaks a lot easier. Initially, the weight of the leash attached to the puppy's collar can feel strange, and the restrictions presented by a leash can be frustrating. Leash training will help your puppy work through these frustrations quickly.

Your puppy won't be taking long walks at first (see page 55 for exercise requirements), but as they get older, your walks will last longer, and you'll likely explore novel environments and walking paths. Distractions out in the world will act as challenges during leash training, so building a solid foundation in a more controlled environment first (like your backyard) will help you and your puppy be more successful out in the world. The beginning stages of leash training can be accomplished over a couple of days, but proofing the behavior so that it's reliable around various distractions can take several weeks.

What You'll Need

To start leash training your puppy, you'll need to purchase the appropriate equipment.

▶ **Regular collar.** A collar that fits well with a buckle or snap is preferred. If your puppy has a narrow head (as breeds like greyhounds and whippets do) or if they're good at slipping out of their collar, you may want to consider either attaching the leash to a body harness or using a martingale collar. Martingale collars are mostly nylon with a small section that cinches so that when your puppy pulls or backs up, the collar tightens, preventing them from escaping. It is not the same as a choke chain or pinch collar, which I don't recommend, as they're aversive and work by inflicting discomfort and pain on the puppy when it pulls.

- ▶ **Body harness.** These are recommended for small dogs who may not tolerate pressure on their trachea, dogs who readily slip out of their collars, or dogs who pull. I recommend a "front-clip harness" (where the leash attaches in the front at the dog's chest rather than in back) because you can use it to interrupt and redirect the dog's momentum if it tries to pull against the leash. A back-clip harness removes pressure from the dog's neck but doesn't redirect pulling—in fact, it makes it more comfortable for the dog to lean into the harness and pull against you.

- ▶ **Leash.** Choose a cheap leash at first, as your puppy may chew through it. The leash should fit comfortably in your hand and be thinner for a smaller dog, wider for a larger dog. Six feet is the standard leash length and is better for everyday walking than a short "tab" leash or a long line.

- ▶ **Treats.** Reward your puppy when they walk politely on a loose leash! It's helpful to store these treats in a treat pouch clipped to your pants or worn around your waist for easy, hands-free access and storage.

What to Do

In order to train your puppy to walk on a loose leash, you first need to teach them what that looks like and reinforce them for being in the desired position. I like to set myself up by holding the handle of my dog's leash in one hand and positioning my dog on the opposite side of my body. So if I want my dog on my right-hand side, I hold the handle of the leash in my left hand so that the body of the leash travels across the front of my body. That way, I can feed treats with my right hand (the hand closest to my dog) when they're precisely where I want them without any awkward twisting.

Start off by holding a treat in your fingers and putting it directly in front of your puppy's nose (you'll likely have to bend down to do this). Leading your puppy with this treat at their nose, take one step forward and feed them a treat at your side. It's important that you feed the treat when your puppy is in the position where you want them to walk. Repeat this exercise several times, and then try walking forward three steps, continuing to lead your puppy with your treat lure and feeding them in position when your steps are completed.

Once your dog can do this with no problem, raise your treat up three or four inches, or until it's at your knee. Walk forward one step in this position, then feed the treat when the puppy is in the correct spot. If your dog can maintain a loose leash with your treat up higher, try walking forward three steps before feeding the treat. Continue to gradually bring your treat lure higher up your leg until you reach your hip. Every time you move your treat higher up your leg, go back to taking only one step before rewarding your puppy. Whenever you make one aspect of the exercise harder (like moving the treat higher), you'll want to make another aspect easier for your puppy (like taking fewer steps).

Once you can walk three steps with your treat hand at your hip while your puppy maintains slack in the leash, remove the treat from your hand. Keep your hand in a similar position at your hip, but leave it empty. Walk forward one step before retrieving a treat from your pocket or pouch and offering it to your puppy. You're no longer luring your puppy forward with a treat, but you still want to reward them for taking successful steps forward on a loose leash. As your puppy is successful, gradually increase the number of steps you take before you offer the reward.

Whenever your puppy makes a mistake and rushes forward or pulls on the leash, stop your walk and ignore them until they return slack to the leash. Make it clear to your puppy from the beginning that the walk can only continue when there's slack in the leash; any tension or pulling will stop the walk and, thus, the dog's ability to explore. Be consistent with this expectation.

Bring in the Experts

While dog training can be simple, it doesn't always go as planned. If you're struggling to achieve success in your training, don't hesitate to contact a professional for guidance. If you notice any behaviors that concern you, such as fear, aggression, anxiety, or antisocial behavior, contact a trainer as soon as possible. Remember, the more your puppy practices a behavior, the more challenging it becomes to modify.

What to Look for in a Trainer

Dog training is a largely unregulated profession, which means that anybody can proclaim themselves a trainer and charge money for their services. Whether you're looking at an individual trainer or group training classes, don't be afraid to ask about their philosophy, tools, and techniques. Do they use shock or prong collars? Do they recommend leash corrections or other aversive devices, such as spray bottles or noise cans, to interrupt unwanted behavior? These are all red flags for potentially harmful, punitive training practices. There is no reason to intimidate or inflict pain upon your puppy in order to train them.

Dog training requires skill and a sound knowledge base, so it's not enough that someone has worked with dogs their entire lives or understands dogs well; they need to be educated and committed to continuous learning. Look for a trainer who is well educated in humane, science-based training and employs positive reinforcement. Check that they're certified, and then look up that certification online to see what it entails.

Types of Training Services

There are various training services available to dog owners. Let's look at the pros and cons of each one so you can determine which is the best fit for you and your puppy.

Group Training Classes

Classes are a great way to get your puppy out of the house to meet new people and dogs. Having an instructor teach you training techniques and guide you when you struggle can save you countless hours of frustration and keep your puppy from getting confused. Additionally, a group class can help keep you motivated and give you incentive to train with your puppy regularly.

Look for classes that offer programs for puppies during their socialization period. Most classes will require that your puppy have their first vaccinations before entering the group but will understand that the vaccination series is likely not complete. The earlier you can enroll your puppy in a class geared toward socialization, the better. Remember, during this period, your puppy is naïve and curious, creating associations with things they're experiencing, and what better way to capitalize on this than in a room full of puppies in the same stage of life?

Puppy classes can range from about $150 to $250, depending on the length of the class and how many weeks it runs. Look for a class led by a certified, professional dog trainer. It should be held in a clean, safe facility with easy-to-disinfect flooring (carpet is a big no-no), and the facility should be disinfected before puppies enter to reduce the risk of disease spreading. When your puppy is older, you may choose to enroll in further classes focusing on varying levels of obedience or sports.

Group classes may not be the best choice if your puppy is fearful of other dogs or people, or if you have very specific training goals. Classes generally follow a structured curriculum, which may not necessarily apply to the exact problem you're currently dealing with. Don't let this discourage you! Your dog may just need a different training approach. Private lessons or classes focused on dog reactivity or fear would be most beneficial. You can even look for in-home or online consultations if bringing your puppy to an unfamiliar environment is too overwhelming.

Private Training

Signing up for private training with your puppy is a good idea if you have specific training concerns that may or may not be addressed in a group class or behavior concerns such as aggression, anxiety, or fear. If you notice any worrisome behavior from your puppy, don't hesitate to contact a trainer for advice. Many of these issues have a better success rate with early intervention. Private training is generally more expensive than group training, ranging from approximately $50 to $150 per hour. Trainers often offer private lessons at their facilities as well as in your home. You can expect to pay more if the trainer must come to you, but that may be worth it if your puppy is fearful of new environments or only displays a certain problem behavior at home. Depending on the trainer, they may have specific vaccination requirements, so be sure to ask.

Distance Consulting

Distance consulting is a service to consider if you don't have access to a certified positive-reinforcement dog trainer locally. Many trainers offer their services remotely, analyzing video, running sessions through teleconferencing platforms, and providing online coaching. Distance consulting is a good option for puppies who might be fearful or struggle in a novel environment, and it's a great approach for rehabilitating dogs with separation anxiety. As with the other services, look for a trainer with the appropriate education and certifications. Distance consulting should cost roughly the same as private training sessions ($50 to $150 per hour).

Resources

ClickerTraining.com (website of Karen Pryor, one of the founders of clicker training)

CompanionAnimalPsychology.com (website of psychologist and dog trainer Zazie Todd)

The Culture Clash: A Revolutionary New Way of Understanding the Relationship Between Humans and Domestic Dogs by Jean Donaldson

Don't Shoot the Dog!: The New Art of Teaching and Training by Karen Pryor

Puppy Start Right: Foundation Training for the Companion Dog by Dr. Kenneth Martin and Debbie Martin

Reaching the Animal Mind: Clicker Training and What It Teaches Us About All Animals by Karen Pryor

References

Chapter 2

Cafazzo, Simona, et al. "Dominance in Relation to Age, Sex, and Competitive Contexts in a Group of Free-Ranging Domestic Dogs." *Behavioral Ecology* 21, no. 3 (May–June 2010): 443–55. doi:10.1093/beheco/arq001.

Coren, Stanley. "Canine Dominance: Is the Concept of the Alpha Dog Valid?" *Psychology Today.* July 20, 2010. psychologytoday.com/us/blog/canine-corner/201007/canine-dominance-is-the-concept-the-alpha-dog-valid.

Gibeault, Stephanie. "Strategies to Help Manage Cognitive Decline in Senior Dogs." American Kennel Club. August 1, 2017. akc.org/expert-advice/health/manage-cognitive-decline-in-senior-dogs.

Todd, Zazie. "What Is Positive Punishment in Dog Training?" *Companion Animal Psychology* (blog). October 25, 2017. companionanimalpsychology.com/2017/10/what-is-positive-punishment-in-dog.html.

Veterinary Practice News. "Study: Early Separation from Litter Increases Chances of Behavioral Problems." August 24, 2011. veterinarypracticenews.com/study-early-separation -from-litter-increases-chances-of-behavioral-problems.

Chapter 3

Association of American Feed Control Officials. "Ingredients– Making Pet Food." Accessed March 24, 2020. petfood.aafco .org/Ingredients-Making-Pet-Food.

Axelsson, Erik, et al. "The Genomic Signature of Dog Domesti- cation Reveals Adaptation to a Starch-Rich Diet." *Nature* 495 (January 23, 2013): 360–4. doi:10.1038/nature11837.

Coates, Jennifer. "Are You Feeding Your Dog the Right Amount?" PetMD. Accessed March 24, 2020. petmd.com /blogs/nutritionnuggets/dr-coates/2015/july/are-you -feeding-your-dog-right-amount-32905.

Coates, Jennifer. "Can Dogs Stay Healthy on a Vegetarian Diet?" PetMD. Accessed March 24, 2020. petmd.com/blogs /nutritionnuggets/jcoates/2014/jan/can-dogs-stay-healthy -on-a-vegetarian-diet-31188.

Fell, Andy. "Homemade Dog Food Recipes Can Be Risky Business, Study Finds." *UC Davis News*. July 15, 2003. ucdavis.edu/news/homemade-dog-food-recipes-can-be -risky-business-study-finds.

Food and Drug Administration. "FDA's Advice: Know the Risks of Feeding Raw Foods to Your Pets." June 30, 2014. wayback.archive-it.org/7993/20190423044315/fda.gov/ ForConsumers/ConsumerUpdates/ucm403350.htm.

Freeman, Lisa M., et al. "What Every Pet Owner Should Know About Food Allergies." Clinical Nutrition Service of Cummings

Veterinary Medical Center at Tufts University. January 27, 2017. vetnutrition.tufts.edu/2017/01/food-allergies.

Gallagher, Ashley. "6 Tips for Choosing Healthy Puppy Food." PetMD. Accessed March 24, 2020. petmd.com/dog/centers /nutrition/slideshows/tips-for-choosing-puppy-food.

Heinze, Cailin. "Breed Specific vs All Breed Diets." Clinical Nutrition Service of Cummings Veterinary Medical Center at Tufts University. August 2, 2018. vetnutrition.tufts.edu/2018 /08/breed-specific-diets.

Heinze, Cailin. "Vegan Dogs—A Healthy Lifestyle or Going Against Nature?" Clinical Nutrition Service of Cummings Veterinary Medical Center at Tufts University. July 21, 2016. vetnutrition.tufts.edu/2016/07/vegan-dogs-a-healthy -lifestyle-or-going-against-nature.

Joffe, Daniel J., and Daniel P. Schlesinger. "Preliminary Assessment of the Risk of *Salmonella* Infection in Dogs Fed Raw Chicken Diets." *Canadian Veterinary Journal* 43, no. 6 (June 2002): 441–2.

Lee, Elizabeth. "Raw Dog Food: Dietary Concerns, Benefits, and Risks." WebMD. Accessed March 24, 2020. pets.webmd .com/dogs/guide/raw-dog-food-dietary-concerns-benefits -and-risks#1.

Mansourian, Erika. "Puppy Feeding Fundamentals." American Kennel Club. July 15, 2019. akc.org/expert-advice/health /puppy-feeding-fundamentals.

PetMD. "The Importance of Water for Dog Nutrition." Accessed March 24, 2020. petmd.com/dog/nutrition/evr_dg_the _importance_of_water.

Purina. "The Healthy Dog Weight and Body Condition." Accessed March 24, 2020. purina.co.uk/dogs/health-and -nutrition/exercise-and-weight-management/dog-body -condition-tool.

Stilwell, Natalie. "Obesity in Dogs: Symptoms, Causes and What to Do About It." PetMD. Last modified December 9, 2019. petmd.com/dog/conditions/digestive/c_multi_obesity.

Xu, Elizabeth. "Signs and Symptoms of Bloat in Dogs." PetMD. Accessed March 24, 2020. petmd.com/dog/conditions /digestive/signs-and-symptoms-bloat-dogs.

Chapter 4

Alt, Kimberly. "Why Do Dogs Like Squeaky Toys?" *Canine Journal.* Last modified January 4, 2019. caninejournal.com /why-do-dogs-like-squeaky-toys.

Dog Health. "Tug of War." Accessed March 24, 2020. doghealth.com/fun-and-play/games/1922-tug-of-war-1.

Gibeault, Stephanie. "Zoomies: Why Your Dog Gets Hyper & Runs in Circles." American Kennel Club. January 29, 2019. akc.org/expert-advice/lifestyle/what-are-zoomies.

iSpeakDog (blog). "Predatory Behavior." Accessed March 24, 2020. ispeakdog.org/predatory-behavior.html.

Kennel Club. "Puppy and Dog Walking Tips." Accessed March 24, 2020. thekennelclub.org.uk/getting-a-dog-or-puppy/general -advice-about-caring-for-your-new-puppy-or-dog/puppy-and -dog-walking.

National Sleep Foundation. "How Many Hours Do Dogs Sleep Each Day?" Accessed March 24, 2020. sleep.org/articles /how-much-do-dogs-sleep.

Sarkar, Rohan, et al. "Scavengers Can Be Choosers: A Study on Food Preference in Free-Ranging Dogs." *Applied Animal Behaviour Science* 216 (July 2019): 38–44. doi:10.1016 /j.applanim.2019.04.012.

Chapter 5

American Veterinary Dental College. "What is an Anesthesia Free Pet Dental Cleaning?" Accessed March 24, 2020. afd .avdc.org/what-is-an-anesthesia-free-dental-cleaning.

Clark, Mike. "How to Tell if Your Dog Has Hair or Fur and Why it Matters." Dogtime. Accessed March 24, 2020. dogtime .com/reference/dog-grooming/65235-how-to-tell-if-your -dog-has-hair-or-fur-and-what-it-means.

Fanslau, Jill. "7 Common Bath-Time Mistakes Pet Owners Make." PetMD. Accessed March 24, 2020. petmd.com/dog /slideshows/7-common-bath-time-mistakes-pet-owners -make.

Meyers, Harriet. "How to Trim Your Dog's Nails Safely." American Kennel Club. April 1, 2020. akc.org/expert-advice /health/how-to-trim-dogs-nails-safely.

New Haven Pet Hospital. "Smelly Paws? The True Story About Canine 'Frito Feet.'" March 20, 2019. newhaven pethospital.com/blog/smelly-paws-the-true-story-about -canine-frito-feet.

Chapter 6

American Heartworm Society. "Heartworm Basics." Accessed March 24, 2020. heartwormsociety.org/pet-owner-resources /heartworm-basics.

American Veterinary Medical Association. "Microchipping of Animals FAQ." Accessed March 24, 2020. avma.org /microchipping-animals-faq.

Atwell, Rick. "Overview of Tick Paralysis." *Merck Veterinary Manual.* Accessed March 24, 2020. merckvetmanual.com /nervous-system/tick-paralysis/overview-of-tick-paralysis.

Brooks, Wendy. "Ear Infections (Yeast Otitis) in Dogs." Veterinary Partner. Last modified September 25, 2018. veterinarypartner.vin.com/default.aspx?pid=19239&id =8621491.

Canadian Veterinary Medical Association. "Scooting May Indicate Anal Gland Problems." October 23, 2012. canadianveterinarians.net/documents/scooting-may -indicate-anal-gland-problems.

Centers for Disease Control and Prevention. "Dipylidium FAQs." Last modified January 10, 2012. cdc.gov/parasites /dipylidium/faqs.html.

Centers for Disease Control and Prevention. "How Ticks Spread Disease." Last modified April 9, 2019. cdc.gov/ticks /life_cycle_and_hosts.html.

Centers for Disease Control and Prevention. "Toxocariasis: Epidemiology & Risk Factors." Last modified September 3, 2019. cdc.gov/parasites/toxocariasis/epi.html.

Coates, Jennifer. "What to Do If Your Dog Swallowed Something They Shouldn't Have." Last modified October 7, 2019. petmd.com/dog/emergency/common-emergencies /e_dg_swallowed_objects.

Dangerfield, Katie. "Caring for Your Animal: Is Pet Insurance Worth the Cost?" *Global News.* March 11, 2018. globalnews .ca/news/4068150/pet-insurance-is-it-worth-the-cost.

Ford, Richard B., et al. "2017 AAHA Canine Vaccination Guidelines." American Animal Hospital Association. October 2017. aaha.org/globalassets/02-guidelines/canine-vaccination

/vaccination_recommendation_for_general_practice
_table.pdf.

Kansas State University Veterinary Health Center. "Common Intestinal Parasites in Cats and Dogs." Accessed March 24, 2020. vet.k-state.edu/vhc/services/phc/common-parasites .html.

Kramer, David F. "How Dangerous Are Fleas?" PetMD. Accessed March 24, 2020. petmd.com/dog/parasites/how -dangerous-are-fleas.

Paddock, Arliss. "Spaying and Neutering Your Puppy or Adult Dog: Questions and Answers." American Kennel Club. June 14, 2018. akc.org/expert-advice/health/spaying-and-neutering -your-dog-faqs.

PetMD. "Hearing Loss in Dogs." Accessed March 24, 2020. petmd.com/dog/conditions/ears/c_multi_deafness.

Pet Poison Helpline. "Poison List." Accessed March 24, 2020. petpoisonhelpline.com/poisons.

Racine, Elizabeth. "Dog Ear Infections: Symptoms, Causes, Treatment, and Prevention." American Kennel Club. September 2, 2019. akc.org/expert-advice/health/dog -ear-infections.

Thomas, Jennifer E. "Lice of Dogs." *Merck Veterinary Manual.* Accessed March 24, 2020. merckvetmanual.com/dog-owners /skin-disorders-of-dogs/lice-of-dogs.

Veterinary Information Network Dermatology Consultants. "Atopic Dermatitis in Dogs." Veterinary Partner. Last modified April 26, 2018. veterinarypartner.vin.com/default .aspx?pid=19239&id=4951973.

WebMD. "Roundworms in Dogs." Last modified October 24, 2018. pets.webmd.com/dogs/roundworms-dogs#1.

WebMD. "Slideshow: 25 Most Popular Dog Breeds and Their Health Issues." Last modified February 13, 2020. webmd .com/dogs/ss/slideshow-dog-breed-health-problems.

Chapter 7

AKC staff. "Dog Boarding: What to Know & What to Look for When Boarding Your Dog." American Kennel Club. February 24, 2020. akc.org/expert-advice/home-living /dog-boarding-tips-for-boarding-your-dog.

American Society for the Prevention of Cruelty to Animals. "Separation Anxiety." Accessed March 24, 2020. aspca.org /pet-care/dog-care/common-dog-behavior-issues /separation-anxiety.

American Veterinary Society of Animal Behavior. "AVSAB Position Statement on Puppy Socialization." Accessed March 24, 2020. avsab.org/wp-content/uploads/2019/01 /Puppy-Socialization-Position-Statement-FINAL.pdf.

Animal Humane Society. "Counter Conditioning and Desensitization." Accessed March 24, 2020. animalhumane society.org/behavior/counter-conditioning-and -desensitization.

Bowman, Amy, et al. "The Effect of Different Genres of Music on the Stress Levels of Kennelled Dogs." *Physiology and Behavior* 171 (March 15, 2017): 207-15. doi:10.1016 /j.physbeh.2017.01.024.

de Cardenas, Cecilia. "Extreme Fear and Anxiety in Dogs." PetMD. Last modified August 6, 2019. petmd.com/dog /conditions/behavioral/c_dg_fears_phobia_anxiety.

Cattet, Jennifer. "Learning Theory Basics, Part 1–Classical Conditioning in Dogs: Beyond the Training Session." *Pet Tutor* (blog). February 24, 2014. blog.smartanimaltraining .com/2014/02/24/classical-conditioning-in-dogs-beyond -the-training-session.

Central California Society for the Prevention of Cruelty to Animals. "Leaving a Dog Home Alone? Here Are 3 Steps to Follow." October 26, 2017. ccspca.com/blog-spca/education /leaving-a-dog-home-alone.

DeMartini, Malena. "About Dog Separation Anxiety." Accessed March 24, 2020. malenademartini.com/about /dog-separation-anxiety.

Gilpatrick, John. "8 Ways to Calm Your Dog Naturally." PetMD. Last modified July 17, 2019. petmd.com/8-ways-calm-your -dog-naturally.

Humane Society of the United States. "How to Housetrain Your Dog or Puppy." Accessed March 24, 2020. humane society.org/resources/how-housetrain-your-dog-or-puppy.

Kahler, Susan. "Separation Anxiety Calls for Specific Diagnosis, Treatment." American Veterinary Medical Association. August 29, 2018. avma.org/javma-news/2018-09-15 /separation-anxiety-calls-specific-diagnosis-treatment.

Landsberg, Gary. "Behavior Modification in Dogs." *Merck Veterinary Manual.* Accessed March 24, 2020. merck vetmanual.com/dog-owners/behavior-of-dogs/behavior -modification-in-dogs.

Madson, Cathy. "Choosing the Best Daycare for Your Dog." Preventive Vet. Last modified February 27, 2020. preventivevet.com/dogs/how-to-choose-a-dog-daycare.

Moore, Timothy. "How Much Does Doggy Day Care Cost? How to Decide if It's Worth the Price." *The Penny Hoarder.* Last modified July 5, 2017. thepennyhoarder.com/save-money /is-doggy-day-care-worth-it-how-to-pick-the-right-place -for-your-pooch.

Sinn, Leslie. "Puppy & Kitten Socialization." *Clinician's Brief.* December 2019. cliniciansbrief.com/article/puppy-kitten -socialization.

Todd, Zazie. "What Is Desensitization and Counter-Conditioning in Dog Training?" *Companion Animal Psychology* (blog). July 11, 2018. companionanimalpsychology.com/2018/07/what-is -desensitization-and-counter.html.

Yin, Sophia. "Puppy Socialization: Stop Fear Before it Starts." *CattleDog Publishing* (blog). September 9, 2011. drsophiayin .com/blog/entry/puppy-socialization-stop-fear-before -it-starts.

Index

Acknowledgments

Writing a book has been a lifelong dream of mine. This experience has been nothing less than surreal. I feel so grateful that not only did I get to write a book, I also got to write about what I'm most passionate about: dogs. With this dream in mind, I could not have accomplished this project without the encouragement of many people.

Thank you to the entire team at Rockridge Press, for believing in me and my training abilities and making this first-time author's writing experience so effortless and enjoyable! I will forever be grateful for this opportunity.

To my supportive sister-in-law, Christa Charbonneau. Thank you for your unconditional encouragement and persistent attitude, especially when it came to tough chapters and book deadlines.

To my dad, for instilling a deep love and respect for dogs in me from a young age, for demonstrating to me what the human-animal bond looks like, and for your genuine interest in my work, no matter what it may be.

Thank you to my family, near and far, for not giving me a hard time when writing time overflowed into family time and for supporting me even when it was challenging to do so.

To my girls, for being my biggest cheerleaders, always and forever.

To my husband, Chris, for your unconditional support, even when my ambitions are completely crazy! You manage to always have my back. Thank you for allowing me to dream but at the same time keeping me grounded.

To all of the inspiring people who have encouraged me and helped me become a successful dog trainer: Jeanne Shaw,

Carolyn Clarke and the Karen Pryor Academy Alumni, Jean Donaldson and the Academy group, and my Sit Pretty team.

To the dogs who have taught me to respect and communicate more clearly with them. Buster, for showing me there is a better way to reach the animal mind. Kaslo, for teaching me patience, empathy, and how to adjust my expectations.

And finally, to you, the reader. Thank you for picking up this book. By doing so, you have already made the first step in becoming an informed dog owner. Thank you for wanting to do the best for your new family member, and thank you for giving me the opportunity to assist you in your journey!

About the Author

Vanessa Charbonneau is a registered veterinary technician and certified dog trainer. Her passion for dog training began at an early age, as she grew up living with working police dogs. Currently, Vanessa is in her seventh year as a dog trainer, specifically working with behavioral cases. As a lifelong learner, Vanessa is devoted to furthering her understanding of dog behavior, spending much of her time enrolled in courses and attending seminars both nationally and internationally. Vanessa works tirelessly to educate dog owners on the best practices of the power of positive reinforcement while using humane, science-based training methods. She is proud to be one of the first trainers in Northern British Columbia to become accredited by the BC SPCA's AnimalKind program. Vanessa lives in Prince George, BC, with her husband, their two daughters, and one dog.

CPSIA information can be obtained
at www.ICGtesting.com
Printed in the USA
JSHW021927120720
6643JS00007B/26

9 781647 392635